1 d4 d5 2 c4 c6

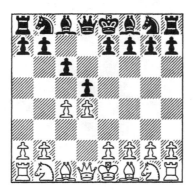

T0163072

To my parents.

The Slav

CHESS PRESS OPENING GUIDES

Other titles in this series include:

1 901259 05 6	Caro-Kann Advance	Byron Jacobs
1 901259 03 X	Dutch Leningrad	Neil McDonald
1 901259 02 1	Scandinavian	John Emms
1 901259 06 4	Sicilian Closed	Daniel King
1 901259 01 3	Sicilian Taimanov	James Plaskett
1 901259 04 8	Spanish Exchange	Andrew Kinsman

Chess Press Opening Guides

The Slav

Matthew Sadler

The Chess Press, Brighton

First published in 1997 by Chess Press, a division of First Rank Publishing

Copyright © 1997 Matthew Sadler

Reprinted 2003

The right of Matthew Sadler to be identified as the author of this work has been asserted in accordance with the Copyrights, Designs and Patents Act 1988.

All rights reserved. No part of this publication may be reproduced, stored in a retrieval system or transmitted in any form or by any means, electronic, electrostatic, magnetic tape, photocopying, recording or otherwise, without prior permission of the publisher.

British Library Cataloguing-in-Publication Data
A catalogue record for this book is available from the British Library.

ISBN 1 901259 00 5

Distributed in North America by The Globe Pequot Press, P.O Box 480, 246 Goose Lane, Guilford, CT 06437-0480.

All other sales enquiries should be directed to Everyman Chess, Gloucester Publishers plc, Gloucester Mansions, 140A Shaftesbury Avenue, London WC2H 8HD
tel: 020 7539 7600 fax: 020 7379 4060
email: info@everymanchess.com
website: www.everymanchess.com

Everyman is the registered trade mark of Random House Inc. and is used in this work under license from Random House Inc.

Cover design by Ray Shell Design.
Production by Navigator Guides.

CONTENTS

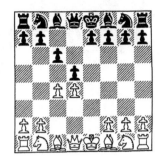

1 d4 d5 2 c4 c6

BIBLIOGRAPHY

Books

Encyclopaedia of Chess Openings vol. D (ECO), Sahovski Informator 1987
Batsford Chess Openings 2 (BCO), Kasparov & Keene (Batsford 1989)
Winning with the Slav, Schipkov & Markov (Batsford 1994)
The Slav for the Tournament Player, Flear (Batsford 1988)

Periodicals

Informator
ChessBase Magazine
New In Chess Yearbook
British Chess Magazine
Chess Monthly

INTRODUCTION

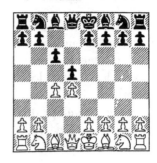

1 d4 d5 2 c4 c6

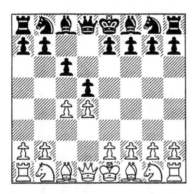

The skill of preparing an opening is frequently misunderstood: many players (including some strong grandmasters) believe that to play an opening well, it is necessary to analyse a great many variations; that no preparation is complete without at least one queen sacrifice and that to stop before move 20 is akin to criminal negligence. I know from experience that the sheer volume of opening theory can be overwhelming, and this is especially true for the non-professional player who has little time to keep up with the latest fashions.

And yet, having been a professional player now for six years, I know that I have won more games from 'nor-mal' openings than from any 30-move piece of analysis (and it's not because I haven't done any!). The brilliant 'I had this position after move 80 on my board at home' games that we see in magazines are the exceptions: beautiful, treasured by every chessplayer, but very, very rare. Chess is a sport and most games are a struggle, and we win games because we fight harder than our opponents, or because we understand the position better.

In my opinion, opening preparation can be successfully reduced to three simple steps:

1. Knowing the main aim of our opening.

2. Knowing the value of move-orders.

3. Understanding typical positions.

Therefore, let's apply these ideas to the Slav.

Opening Aims
With 2 c4, White challenges the black centre. The natural 2...e6, allowing Black to develop his kingside pieces, has the drawback of blocking the light-squared bishop inside the pawn chain. 2...c6 aims to hold the centre, to develop the light-squared bishop

outside the pawn chain, and then to play ...e7-e6 and conclude the black development. However, the course of chess ideas, like love, never runs smoothly! Black must be careful when he develops his light-squared bishop: after 1 d4 d5 2 c4 c6 3 ♘f3 ♘f6 4 ♘c3

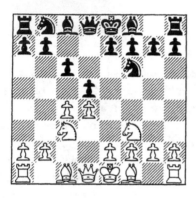

Black would like to play 4...♗f5, but he will have great difficulty defending b7 after 5 cxd5 cxd5 6 ♕b3!

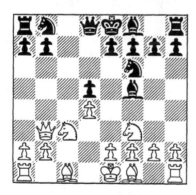

Now 6...♕b6 loses a pawn to 7 ♘xd5 ♕xb3 8 ♘xf6+ exf6 9 axb3 and 6...b6 weakens the queenside light-squares too much: 7 e4! dxe4 8 ♘e5 e6 (to stop ♕xf7+ mate) 9 ♗b5+ ♘fd7 10 g4 ♗g6 11 h4!, intending h4-h5, trapping the bishop. The general rule is

that Black can only play a quick ...♗f5 if he can successfully defend b7 with his queen. Thus, 1 d4 d5 2 c4 c6 3 ♘f3 ♘f6 4 e3 ♗f5

is fine for Black since 5 cxd5 cxd5 6 ♕b3 can easily be met by 6...♕c7; however 1 d4 d5 2 c4 c6 3 ♘c3 ♘f6 4 e3 ♗f5?!

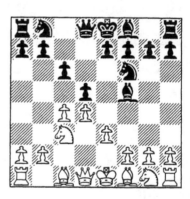

5 cxd5 cxd5 6 ♕b3 is not good, since 6...♕c7 loses a pawn to 7 ♘xd5. So how can Black carry out his main idea? Black either has to stop White from playing ♕b3, or he has to find a good way to defend b7. This is a typical opening dilemma: whether to prevent an opponent's threat directly, or whether to arrange the pieces in such a way that the threat is nullified.

The main line of the Slav runs 1 d4 d5 2 c4 c6 3 ♘f3 ♘f6 4 ♘c3 dxc4.

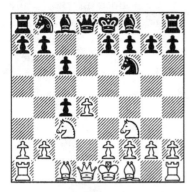

First, Black wins a pawn and threatens ...b7-b5, making this gain permanent. Second, the b3-square is cunningly taken away from the queen, which means that White cannot attack b7, and hence that ...♗f5 becomes possible. While White recaptures the c4-pawn, Black will develop the light-squared bishop to f5 or g4 and will be looking to complete his kingside development: 5 a4 (surrounding the c-pawn by preventing ...b7-b5) 5...♗f5 6 ♘e5 (intending ♘xc4) or 6 e3 (intending ♗xc4) 6...e6 are the main lines. So far I have been very enthusiastic about Black's strategy, but now I have to reveal the downside of his play. This sort of schizophrenia is necessary when you play both sides of the Slav, as I do!

4...dxc4 relinquishes control of e4, which makes it easier for White to cramp Black with two central pawns on d4 and e4. But White must be careful that his pawns do not become weaknesses as Black first immobilises, then attacks them. The bottom line is that the player who has the better understanding of the line will get the best results with either colour.

The second idea is to play 1 d4 d5 2 c4 c6 3 ♘f3 ♘f6 4 ♘c3 a6.

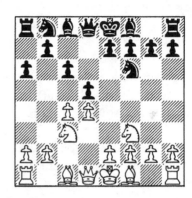

The move 4...a6 was first played in Britain by Grandmaster Jon Levitt, but it is Grandmaster Julian Hodgson who has upheld this variation at the highest level, and introduced the most significant ideas.

The original idea of 1 d4 d5 2 c4 c6 3 ♘f3 ♘f6 4 ♘c3 a6 was to meet ♕b3 with ...b7-b5, moving the pawn to a protected square. However, ways were found to exploit the drawbacks of ...b7-b5: the dark-square weaknesses on c5, b6, a5 and the slightly exposed black queenside. Then, in a brilliant piece of unstereotyped thinking, Hodgson realised that ...a7-a6 could allow the rook to defend b7 from a7. No one had dared to play such a strange move before, but Julian did, and this has made some previously dodgy lines completely viable.

However, although avoiding ...d5xc4 helps to prevent e2-e4, Black's position is less dynamic than in the ...d5xc4 lines, as it is much harder to break against White's centre with

...c6-c5 and ...e7-e5. My own preference as Black is for the 4...dxc4 lines, as they are richer in content and offer a wider range of possibilities to suit many different styles.

Move-Orders

Move-orders are a much underrated part of opening preparation. Opponents don't always play fair! Imagine the scene: you sit down to play, confident that you know your opening at least as well as your opponent, and what happens? He plays the opening in some unusual move-order, and you emerge a bit dazed to find yourself playing a different line to the one you wanted! And unless you work out your move-orders thoroughly, this will continue to happen, time and time again.

So how can this happen in the Slav?

If you want to play the 4...a6 Slav, then there is nothing that White can do to muddy the water, which is one of the attractions of this line. 4...dxc4 lines, however, require some care. First, White can try to sidestep them by playing an early e2-e3, protecting c4, e.g. 3 ♘c3 ♘f6 4 e3. Black has many reasonable moves here, but none of them fit in with the idea we want to play. The other way for White to play is c4xd5, leading to the Exchange variation; 4...a6 Slav fans should study these positions particularly carefully, since this sort of position is very typical of this line, and there are many transpositions.

Understanding Typical Positions

Well, for this part, read on...

CHAPTER ONE

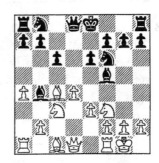

The Old Main Line:
Black plays to prevent e3-e4

1 d4 d5 2 c4 c6 3 ♘f3 ♘f6 4 ♘c3 dxc4 5 a4 ♗f5 6 e3 e6 7 ♗xc4 ♗b4 8 0-0

This traditional system of development for White is especially popular at club level. White quietly recaptures the pawn and puts his king to safety before he starts his plan of e3-e4, to obtain a 'perfect' pawn centre. This chapter examines Black's attempts to prevent White from achieving this goal.

First, we need to ask ourselves a few questions in order to establish our approach:

Question 1: How will White try and achieve e3-e4?

Answer: White has two major approaches:

a) ♕e2. This is the most dangerous idea, which we shall examine first.

b) ♘h4, to remove the bishop on f5, which is helping Black to prevent e3-e4.

Question 2: How can Black fight against ♕e2 and e3-e4?

Answer: Black has three pieces attacking the e4-square: the bishops on b4 and f5 and the knight on f6. When White plays ♕e2 he is supporting the e3-e4 push with only two pieces: the

queen and the knight on c3. However, he will achieve the e3-e4 advance with tempo because the e-pawn attacks the bishop on f5. If Black wants to, he can simply pre-empt this by retreating the bishop to g6, so that e3-e4 no longer attacks the bishop. Now if White plays e3-e4 regardless, Black can win a pawn by playing ...♗xc3 and ...♘xe4.

Question 3: What move-order should I play this in?

Answer: My own favourite has been to play 8...0-0 9 ♕e2 ♗g6; 8...♘bd7 9 ♕e2 ♗g6 is sharper since White can offer a dangerous pawn sacrifice.

Game 1
Richardson-Sadler
Islington Open 1995

This was a crucial game for me: I was leading the Islington Open by only half a point and only a win would guarantee first place. However, even more importantly, only a win would be good enough to pip Keith Arkell for the Leigh Grand Prix!

1 d4 d5 2 c4 c6 3 ♘f3 ♘f6 4 ♘c3 dxc4 5 a4 ♗f5 6 e3 e6 7 ♗xc4 ♗b4

8 0-0 0-0 9 ♕e2 ♗g6 10 ♘e5

10 e4?! ♗xc3! 11 bxc3 ♘xe4 wins a safe pawn. Consequently, White reverts to 'Plan B': he exchanges his knight on f3 for my bishop on g6 and removes an attacker of e4.

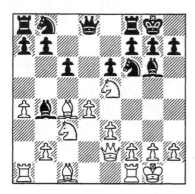

10...♘bd7 11 ♘xg6 hxg6 12 ♖d1

12 e4 ♘b6! wins a pawn as 13 e5 (or 13 ♖d1 ♗xc3 14 bxc3 ♘xc4 15 ♕xc4 ♘xe4) fails to 13...♕xd4 14 ♗xe6 fxe6 15 exf6 ♕xf6 with a clear extra pawn.

12...♕e7!?

An interesting move, though I imagine that it is not the most accurate – for Kramnik's 12...♕a5, see the next game.

13 e4

Wait a minute! Wasn't Black play-ing to prevent e3-e4? Well, since White's aim was to push a pawn within his own territory, it was always unlikely that we could prevent it for ever. However, by resisting for as long as possible, we have forced White to make a concession, namely that he has had to play ♘e5xg6 before being able to play e3-e4. Although White gains the two bishops with this manoeuvre, he exchanges off the piece that would be most affected by the e3-e4 advance; on g6, the bishop has little scope if White can maintain his pawn on e4. Moreover, the departure of the knight from f3 means that White loses some control over the central dark squares, d4 and e5. This last point is seen to great effect in this game.

13...e5 14 d5 ♖ac8!

I spent a great deal of time at this stage and realised that I had to force White to release the tension in the centre and play d5xc6. The explanation for this has a lot to do with the central dark squares: without the d-pawn, I can transfer a knight to e6 (via c5) and exploit the outpost that my pawn on e5 creates on d4. By placing my rook on c8, I was hoping to get my opponent worried about possible threats on the c-file, in order to tempt him into playing d5xc6.

15 ♗g5 ♖fd8 16 dxc6?

Here it is! After this mistake, White has to be very careful to avoid a disadvantage. The correct plan is extremely ingenious. Black has two avenues of pressure: he has possible threats along the c-file and he can develop some pressure against e4 by means of ...♘c5. How can White deal with both these threats? With the manoeuvre 16 ♖d3! ♘c5 17 ♖e3!! On e3, the rook covers e4 and defends the knight on c3 along the rank, thus protecting White's queenside against c-file play. White is slightly better after 16 ♖d3, but the game is still very complicated.

16...bxc6!

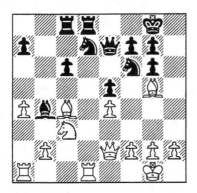

My opponent had underestimated this recapture. Although it weakens Black's queenside pawn structure, Black protects the central light squares, over which he previously had little control due to the exchange of his light-squared bishop. This move is so strong, because White's queenside is so weak: the pawn on a4 gives Black a comfortable slot on b4 for the queen, from which it can attack the a4- and b2-pawns.

17 ♖d3? ♘c5 18 ♖h3? ♘e6!

White's 17th and 18th moves were excessively optimistic as he had no chance of an attack along the h-file. Meanwhile, Black threatens ...♘d4. With his control of the d-file, and White's weakened queenside as a clear target, I believe that Black can already be thinking about victory. During the

game, I was very impressed with White's attitude: realising that his position had worsened considerably, White regrouped and concentrated totally on defence.

19 ♗xe6 ♕xe6 20 ♖d3 ♖xd3 21 ♕xd3 ♕b3 22 ♖b1 ♖b8 23 ♗d2 ♗a5!

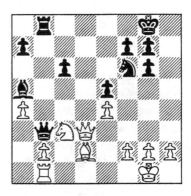

Protecting the d8-square, so that the rook can use either of the open files on the board.

24 f3 ♖d8 25 ♕e2 ♘e8!

Black's knight is the least active of his pieces. The text prepares to bring it to d4 via c7 and e6. When this happens, all of Black's troops will be on their optimal squares.

26 ♗e1 ♘c7 27 ♖c1 ♘e6 28 ♕c2 ♕b6+ 29 ♕f2 ♘d4

Intending 30...♗xc3 31 ♗xc3 ♘e2+ winning the exchange, as 32 ♕xe2 is impossible since the queen is pinned to the king.

30 ♔h1 ♕b3 31 ♖b1 ♖b8 32 h3 ♕c4 33 f4 exf4 34 ♕xf4 ♖e8 35 ♖d1 ♗xc3 36 ♗xc3 ♘e2 37 ♕f3 ♖xe4

The first weak pawn falls.

38 a5 a6 39 ♕d3 ♘xc3 40 ♕xc4 ♖xc4 41 bxc3 ♖c5!

I think that the rook ending is winning now. 41...⊑xc3 42 ⊑d8+ ☗h7 43 ⊑a8 would have regained the a-pawn, but now after 42 ⊑d8+ ☗h7 43 ⊑a8, Black can simply play 43...⊑xa5. **42 ⊑d8+ ☗h7 43 ⊑c8 g5 44 ☗g1 ☗g6 45 ☗f2 ☗f5 46 ⊑c7 f6 47 ⊑xg7 ⊑xa5 48 ☗e3 ⊑e5+ 49 ☗d4 ☗f4 50 ⊑a7 ⊑e6!**

51 ⊑b7

51 ⊑xa6 c5+! wins a rook.
51...☗g3 52 ⊑b2 ⊑e5 53 ⊑b6 c5+ 54 ☗c4 f5 55 ⊑xa6 ☗xg2 56 ⊑g6 f4 57 h4 f3 58 ⊑xg5+ ⊑xg5 59 hxg5 f2 60 ☗xc5 f1♕ 61 c4 ♕f5+ 62 ☗d6 ♕g6+ 0-1

This was a very important game for me, and an instructive example of what both sides should be aiming for in this variation.

Game 2
Karpov-Kramnik
Monte Carlo (blindfold) 1995

1 d4 d5 2 c4 c6 3 ♘f3 ♘f6 4 ♘c3 dxc4 5 a4 ♗f5 6 e3 e6 7 ♗xc4 ♗b4 8 0-0 0-0 9 ♕e2 ♗g6 10 ♘e5 ♘bd7 11 ♘xg6 hxg6 12 ⊑d1 ♕a5!

This move is more active, and probably more logical, than 12...♕e7. While Black is not threatening to win a pawn immediately with 13...♗xc3 due to 14 bxc3 ♕xc3 15 ♗d2 ♕c2 16 ♗d3! ♕b2 17 ⊑db1, winning the queen, it does prevent 13 e4, as with White's centre slightly weakened, Black can get away with taking the pawn: 13...♗xc3 14 bxc3 ♕xc3 15 ♗d2 ♕xd4 (15...♕c2!?) 16 ♗b4 ♕e5 17 ♗xf8 ⊑xf8 when with two pawns for the exchange, Black stands very well. Note that 13 ♘a2 allows 13...♕xa4 14 ♘xb4 ♕xa1 15 ♘a2 (hoping to trap the queen) 15...♕b1!, escaping to f5!

13 ♗d2

Protecting c3, and intending e3-e4,

but...

13...e5 14 d5 ♖ad8

14...cxd5? 15 ♘xd5 ♘xd5 16 ♗xd5 ♕xd5 17 ♗xb4 wins for White.

15 dxc6 bxc6 16 ♗e1 e4!

Securing an outpost on d3 for the knight.

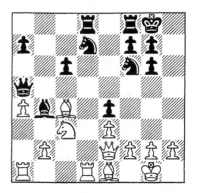

17 ♗b3 ♕e5 18 ♗c2 ♗d6 19 g3 ♘c5 20 ♔g2 ♕f5 21 ♖d2 ♗e5! 22 ♖ad1 ♖b8!

The white queenside is looking very weak.

23 ♗b1 ♗xc3 24 bxc3 ♘xa4 25 ♖a2 ♘b2 26 ♖d2 ♘c4 27 ♖d1 ♘e5 28 h3 ♘f3 29 ♖a4 ♘g5 30 g4 ♕e5 31 ♕c2 ♖fe8 32 ♖xa7 ♘f3

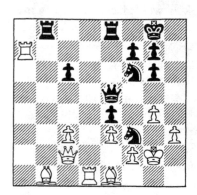

Threatening ...♕h2+. Now Black is just winning.

33 ♕a2 ♕h2+ 34 ♔f1 ♕xh3+ 35 ♔e2 ♘e5 36 ♗c2 ♕xg4+ 37 ♔d2 ♖ed8+ 38 ♔c1 ♖xd1+ 39 ♗xd1 ♕g1 40 ♗d2 ♘d3+ 41 ♔c2 ♖b2+ 0-1

So White's plan of 9 ♕e2 and 10 ♘e5 seems harmless. Let us take a look at the more direct 9 ♘h4.

Game 3
Yusupov-Kramnik
Riga 1995

1 d4 d5 2 c4 c6 3 ♘f3 ♘f6 4 ♘c3 dxc4 5 a4 ♗f5 6 e3 e6 7 ♗xc4 ♗b4 8 0-0 0-0 9 ♘h4!

The most testing idea: White eliminates the bishop on f5 without wasting time on ♕e2.

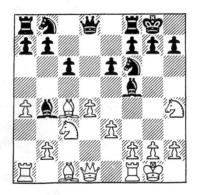

9...♘bd7!?

A typical stratagem: Black's doubled f-pawns will take over the bishop's task of preventing e3-e4.

Question 4: What is wrong with 9...♗g6?

Answer: White can play 10 ♘xg6 hxg6 11 ♕c2!

Question 5: Why is it important to put the queen on c2 and not e2?

Answer: First, the queen neutralises

Black's most active plan of ...♕a5, threatening ...♗xc3. Second, with the queen on c2, Black must be careful that when he plays ...e6-e5 he does not allow ♕xg6! (...e6-e5 has opened up the a2-g8 diagonal and the f7-pawn is now pinned to the king, so Black cannot recapture on g6). Of course, we are dealing with subtle nuances rather than big differences, but it is important to understand them nonetheless.

10 ♘xf5 exf5 11 ♕c2 g6 12 f3 ♕b6

Preventing e3-e4 by attacking the d4-pawn, which has been weakened by the absence of the white knight from f3.

13 ♔h1 ♖ae8 14 ♕f2 c5 15 ♕h4 ♖c8!? 16 ♗a2 ♖fd8 17 ♗d2 ♘f8 18 a5 ♕a6 19 ♖fd1 c4

Shutting out White's light-squared bishop.

20 ♗e1 ♖e8 21 e4 ♗xc3 22 ♗xc3 fxe4 23 d5 ♘8d7 24 ♖d4 ½-½

The draw was agreed in a very murky position.

It is now time to consider the other move-order: 8...♘bd7, intending to meet 9 ♕e2 with 9...♗g6 as above.

Game 4
Ivanchuk-Bareev
Dortmund 1995

1 ♘f3 d5 2 d4 ♘f6 3 c4 c6 4 ♘c3 dxc4 5 a4 ♗f5 6 e3 e6 7 ♗xc4 ♗b4 8 0-0 ♘bd7

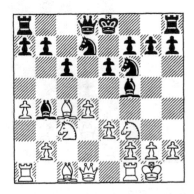

Question 6: What does Black gain from delaying castling?

Answer: 8...♘bd7 is directed against the plan of an early ♘h4, which we saw in Yusupov-Kramnik. After 9 ♘h4, Black will reply 9...♗g6, as 10 ♘xg6 hxg6 is extremely dubious for White. Since Black has not castled, his rook is well placed on the semi-open h-file, pointing towards White's king! Black will play ...♕c7 (attacking h2), castle queenside and then double rooks on the h-file, which is not what White was hoping for when he sensibly (he thought!) took the bishop pair!

So what does White do after 8...♘bd7 9 ♘h4 ♗g6? Give up? Cry? Well, if he's a genius like Ivanchuk, he chooses a third option: he gets sneaky.

9 ♘h4 ♗g6 10 ♗e2!?

White wants to take on g6 only once Black has castled; so he plays a useful consolidating move while he waits for Black to commit his king. The text prevents the bishop on g6 from escaping the knight's attentions by 10...♗h5!? The alternative waiting move, 10 h3, is considered in the next game.

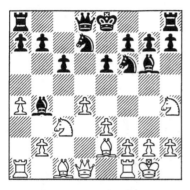

10...0-0

Fans of tactics can investigate 10...♗xc3 11 ♘xg6 (not 11 bxc3 ♘d5 12 ♘xg6 ♘xc3! 13 ♕c2 ♘xe2+ 14 ♕xe2 hxg6, winning a pawn) 11...♗xb2 12 ♘xh8 ♗xa1 13 ♗a3 or 13 ♕c2 (unclear – Ivanchuk) and when they have, I'd be grateful if they could tell me what is going on! However, more positional players can be happy with Bareev's move. Although White's queen will go straight to c2, the bishop is more passive on e2 than on c4: after ...e6-e5, Black no longer has to fear ♕xg6 (in fact he'd be quite pleased to see it!) as the white bishop is not on the a2-g8 diagonal; and this also means that White cannot reply so easily with d4-d5 after ...e6-e5 or ...c6-c5.

11 ♘xg6 hxg6 12 ♕c2

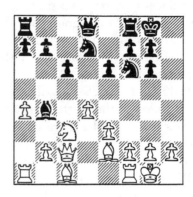

12...♖c8!?

Since the white queen is on the c2, Black tries to inconvenience it by opening the c-file. The immediate 12...c5 would be met by 13 ♘a2!, netting Black's other bishop since 13...♗a5 loses a pawn to 14 dxc5, intending b2-b4. Bareev therefore plays the rook to the c-file in order to facilitate ...c6-c5. The ...c6-c5 break is played less often than ...e6-e5 in the Slav, but it is a typical idea that is well worth remembering.

13 e4!?

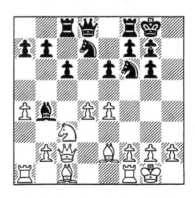

Since White does not want the c-file to be opened, he prepares to meet 13...c5 with 14 d5. If only he still had his bishop on c4! This move introduces a sharp pawn sacrifice that is probably not quite good enough, so 13 ♖d1 was suggested by Ivanchuk as an alternative, when he claims a slight advantage for White. 13...c5 14 d5 exd5 15 ♘xd5 ♘xd5 16 ♖xd5 ♕e7 17 b3! is indeed rather better for White. Black's main problems are the weakness of his light squares and his bishop on b4, which is shut off from the rest of Black's pieces by the pawn on c5. The immediate 13...♕e7 is stronger: 14 e4 (also interesting is 14 b3!?, intending 14...c5 [14...e5 is more sensible] 15 d5 ♗xc3 16 d6! and ♕xc3 with advantage) 14...c5 15 d5 exd5 16 ♘xd5 ♘xd5 17 exd5 (17 ♖xd5 loses the e-pawn to 17 ...♘f6)

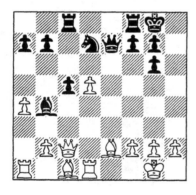

17...c4!, freeing the bishop and preventing White from establishing a light-squared blockade of the queenside with b2-b3 and ♗c4. After 18 ♗xc4, Black can regain the pawn with 18...♘b6 19 b3 ♘xc4 (19...♘xd5 20 ♗b2! [20 ♗xd5 ♖xc2; 20 ♖xd5 ♕e1+!] leaves White more active due to his two raking bishops) 20 bxc4 ♕h4!, when 21 f4 (the only move to save the c-pawn) 21...♖fe8 (22...♖e1+ is now a threat) 22 g3 ♕g4 gives Black danger-

ous play due to his threat of ...♖e2.

13...c5 14 d5 exd5 15 exd5!? ♖e8?!

The start of a series of slight inaccuracies that Ivanchuk exploits brutally. 15...♗xc3 16 bxc3 ♘xd5 17 ♖d1 ♘7f6! 18 ♗f3 (18 c4 ♘b4! unpins) 18...♕e7! is Ivanchuk's recommendation, as 19 ♗xd5 ♘xd5 20 ♖xd5 allows mate after 20...♕e1.

16 ♖d1 c4

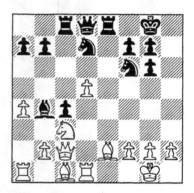

17 d6!

A very strong move: the d6-pawn exposes the light-squared weaknesses in the black position by opening the h1-a8 diagonal and freeing d5 for the knight on c3.

17...♖e6 18 ♗f4 ♕b6 19 ♘b5 ♗c5 20 ♗g3!

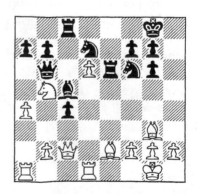

Calmly protecting f2.

20...♘e4 21 ♗g4 f5 22 ♗f3! ♔h7 23 ♘c7 ♖e5 24 ♘d5 ♖xd5 25 ♖xd5 ♘xg3 26 a5 1-0

26 hxg3 would also have won. White is just the exchange up with a winning position.

Game 5
Topalov-Gelfand
Belgrade 1995

1 d4 d5 2 c4 c6 3 ♘f3 ♘f6 4 ♘c3 dxc4 5 a4 ♗f5 6 e3 e6 7 ♗xc4 ♗b4 8 0-0 ♘bd7 9 ♘h4 ♗g6 10 h3!?

Another waiting move. However, Black's bishop has a square!

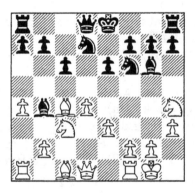

10...♗h5 11 g4 ♘d5!

Black makes a discovered attack by the queen on the knight on h4. Once the knight retreats, Black will again have g6 for his bishop.

12 ♘g2 ♗g6 13 ♘a2 ♗e7?!

Topalov rightly suggests 13...♗d6 14 f3 h5! as an improvement, striking immediately against the exposed king-side pawns.

14 ♕e2 ♘5b6 15 ♗b3 c5 16 ♘c3 0-0 17 a5 cxd4 18 exd4 ♘c8 19 ♘f4

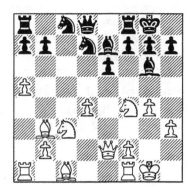

Black's passive play has given White a huge space advantage.

19...♘d6 20 ♘xg6 hxg6 21 ♗f4 ♘e8 22 ♕f3 ♗d6 23 ♗e3 ♘df6 24 g5 ♘h5 25 ♖fd1 ♘c7

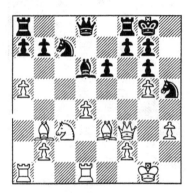

26 ♗c2?!

26 d5! e5 27 ♘e4 (Topalov) would have led to a clear edge for White.

26...f5! 27 h4 b5 28 axb6 axb6 29 ♖xa8 ♕xa8 30 ♕xa8 ♖xa8 31 d5 exd5 32 ♘xd5 ♘xd5 33 ♗b3 ♔f8 34 ♗xd5 ♖a4 35 ♗xb6 ♖xh4 36 ♗c6 ♗e7 37 ♖a1 ♘f4 38 ♖a8+ ♔f7 39 ♗e8+ ♔e6 40 ♖a6 ♔d5 41 ♗f7+ ♔e4 42 ♗e3 ½-½

Instead of 9 ♘h4, White has a more testing plan: 9 ♕e2 and 10 e4!

Game 6
Ivanchuk-Lautier
Linares 1994

1 d4 d5 2 c4 c6 3 ♘f3 ♘f6 4 ♘c3 dxc4 5 a4 ♗f5 6 e3 e6 7 ♗xc4 ♗b4 8 0-0 ♘bd7 9 ♕e2 ♗g6 10 e4!?

This pawn sacrifice is the problem with this move-order.

10...♗xc3

The more restrained 10...0-0 is considered in the next chapter.

11 bxc3 ♘xe4 12 ♗a3!

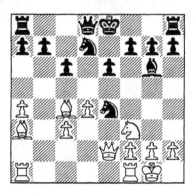

Question 6: What is going on?

Answer: In return for the sacrificed centre pawn, White has gained the two bishops and prevented Black from castling kingside.

Question 7: Can't Black just grab another pawn with 12...♘xc3?

Answer: NO!! 13 ♕b2 (hitting the knight and the pawn on b7) 13...♘xa4 14 ♕b3!, threatening both ♕xa4 and ♗xe6, is horrible for Black.

Question 8: Can't Black just block the a3-f8 diagonal with 12...c5 and then castle kingside?

Answer: This is logical, but 13 dxc5 is awkward, meeting 13...0-0 with 14

c6! and 13...♘exc5 with 14 ♗b5! 0-0 15 ♗xd7 ♘xd7 16 ♗xf8.

Question 9: How then can Black get his king to safety?

Answer: Black can castle queenside instead of kingside.

Question 10: You don't sound very impressed!

Answer: Black's position is horrible! White has a simple and extremely effective plan: a4-a5-a6, softening up the black queenside, and then, after moving the bishop on c4, c3-c4-c5 finishing off the job. In reply, Black must seek to play ...e6-e5 and activate his kingside pawns.

12...♕c7 13 ♖fc1

From c1, the rook protects the c3-pawn and supports the c3-c4-c5 push.

13...0-0-0

13...c5 14 ♘e5! ♘xe5 (14...0-0 15 ♘xg6 wins a piece) 15 dxe5 ♕xe5 (or else White plays f2-f3 and h2-h4, trapping the knight) 16 f3 wins a piece, while 13...♘d6 (blocking the a3-f8 diagonal) 14 ♗xe6! 0-0 (14...fxe6 15 ♕xe6+ is crushing) 15 ♗b3 favours White due to his bishop pair.

14 a5

14...♘d6!?

The young Rumanian player Gabriel Schwartzman tried 14...♖he8 against Razuvaev in Dortmund 1993, but after 15 a6! b6 16 ♘h4 ♘d6 17 ♗b3 e5 18 ♘xg6 hxg6 19 ♕g4! (preventing Black from activating his kingside pawns with...f7-f5 by attacking g6) 19...♔b8 20 ♗xd6! ♕xd6 21 ♗xf7 ♖e7 22 ♕xg6, White stood clearly better. 19...c5 cutting out the bishop on a3, was suggested as an improvement, but after 20 dxc5 bxc5 21 ♖ab1! (preventing 21...♔b8 due to 22 ♗xf7+) 21...♖e7 (defending f7) 22 ♖cd1! (eyeing the knight on d6) the only positive course of action open to Black is to wring the neck of the man who made this suggestion!

15 ♗b3 ♗h5

An idea of Bareev's I believe, trying to inconvenience White by the pin on the knight. Note that 15...♖he8 is met by 16 ♘h4!

16 h3

16 ♕e3 unpinning, and eyeing the a7-pawn, is also interesting.

16...♖he8

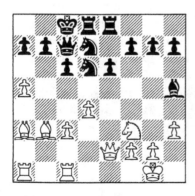

17 a6!

Softening up the protection around the black king.

17...b6 18 c4!

Threatening c4-c5.

18...c5 19 ♗a4 e5 20 dxc5 bxc5 21 ♕e3 ♖e6 22 ♘g5 ♖f6 23 ♗b2 h6 24 ♘e4 ♘xe4 25 ♕xe4 ♖e6

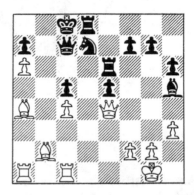

I would not recommend this position to anyone. The game finished:

26 ♖e1 ♗g6 27 ♕a8+ ♕b8 28 ♗xd7+ ♖xd7 29 ♕xb8+ ♔xb8 30 ♖xe5 ♖dd6 31 ♖xc5 ♖xa6 32 ♖xa6 ♖xa6 33 ♗xg7 h5 34 f4 f5 35 ♗e5+ ♔b7 36 ♖c7+ ♔b6 37 ♔h2 ♔a5 38 ♔g3 ♗e8 39 ♔h4 ♔b4 40 g3 ♖g6 41 ♖xa7 ♔xc4 42 ♖a8 ♗c6 43 ♖a3 ♗e8 44 ♖e3 ♔d5 45 ♗f6 ♗d7 46 ♗c3 ♗e6 47 ♗b4 ♗d7 48 ♔xh5 ♖g8 49 ♗c3 ♔d6 50 ♔h6 ♗e6 51 ♔h7 ♖a8 52 ♗b4+ ♔d7 53 ♔g7 ♖a4 54 ♔f6 ♗d5 55 ♗c3 ♗e4 56 g4 fxg4 57 hxg4 ♗c2 58 ♖e7+ ♔d8 59 ♗e5 ♖a6+ 60 ♖e6 ♖xe6+ 61 ♔xe6 ♔e8 62 ♗d6 ♗d1 63 g5 ♗c2 64 f5 1-0

Game 7
Ehlvest-Schwartzman
New York Open 1996

---

1 ♘f3 d5 2 d4 ♘f6 3 c4 c6 4 ♘c3 dxc4 5 a4 ♗f5 6 e3 e6 7 ♗xc4 ♗b4

8 0-0 ♘bd7 9 ♕e2 ♗g6 10 e4 ♗xc3
11 bxc3 ♘xe4 12 ♗a3 ♕c7 13 ♖fc1
0-0-0 14 a5 ♔b8 15 ♗e7!?

An interesting manoeuvre, transferring the bishop to the annoying h2-b8 diagonal. The bishop has already fulfilled its task on a3 by preventing the black king from castling kingside.

15...♖de8 16 ♗h4 ♔a8 17 ♕b2 f5
18 ♘d2 f4 19 f3 ♘xd2 20 ♕xd2
♖hf8 21 ♗f1 e5 22 dxe5 ♖xe5 23 a6

Ehlvest criticises this move, preferring White after 23 ♖a4 ♖d5 24 ♕a2 ♘c5 25 ♖d4. This may well be more accurate, but the essential point is that White will always have very good chances because Black's king is weak and White's bishops are strong.

23...b6 24 ♖a4 ♖d5 25 ♖d4 ♖xd4
26 ♕xd4 ♘c5 27 ♖d1 ♖e8 28 ♗c4
♗c2 29 ♖e1 ♖xe1+ 30 ♗xe1 ♗f5
31 ♗d2 ♕d7 32 ♕xf4 b5 33 ♗f1
♘xa6 34 ♗e3 ♔b7 35 ♗f2 ♗g6 36
h4 c5 37 ♕e3 ♔b6 38 ♔h2 ♕e8 39
♕g5 h6 40 ♕d2 ♕c6 41 ♗g3 ♕f6
42 ♕d7 c4 43 ♗f2+ ♘c5 44 g3!

After a time-scramble and a little confusion, White re-establishes control with this evil little move, which

prepares to activate the light-squared bishop on the long diagonal. 44...♕xf3 loses simply to 45 ♕d6+.

44...a5 45 ♗g2 ♕c6 46 ♕d8+ ♔a6
47 ♕e7 ♘d7 48 f4 ♕c7 49 ♕e6+
♘b6 50 ♕xg6 a4 51 ♕e8 a3 52 ♕f8
a2 53 ♕a3+ ♘a4 54 ♕xa2 ♕d7 55
♗d4 1-0

If this isn't enough to convince you of the danger in accepting the pawn sacrifice, then try this!

> ### Game 8
> ### Hübner-Beliavsky
> *Munich 1994*

1 d4 d5 2 c4 c6 3 ♘c3 ♘f6 4 ♘f3
dxc4 5 a4 ♗f5 6 e3 e6 7 ♗xc4 ♗b4
8 0-0 ♘bd7 9 ♕e2 ♗g6 10 e4 ♗xc3
11 bxc3 ♘xe4 12 ♗a3 ♕c7 13
♖fe1!?

A very aggressive alternative to the old 13 ♖fc1. White sacrifices yet another pawn, reasoning that this will merely open more lines for his pieces.

13...♘xc3

Best and the most critical. 13...0-0-0 was extremely unpleasant for Black in the game Beliavsky-Akopian, Novosibirsk 1993: 14 ♕b2 ♖he8 15 a5 e5 16 ♖ab1 c5 17 ♗f1 f6 and now 18 ♘h4! ♘xc3 19 ♕xc3 exd4 20 ♕b3 ♗xb1 21 ♖xb1 gives White an overwhelming initiative, as Beliavsky pointed out. Clearly in such lines, the king's rook is much more actively placed on e1 than on c1 (as in lines we have seen previously). This is also true of 13...c5, as in Hübner-Hertneck, Munich 1994, when 14 d5! e5 15 ♗d3! ♘ef6 16 ♘xe5 0-0-0 17 ♘xd7 ♖xd7 18 c4 (Hübner) is the (unpleasant) best that Black can hope for.

14 ♕b2 ♘e4 15 a5!?

To break up the black queenside with a5-a6. 15 ♖ac1 is also interesting.

15 ... ♘df6

15...♘d6 (intending ...0-0) is met by 16 ♗xe6! (16 ♕b4 c5! [not 16...♘xc4?? 17 ♕e7 mate] 17 dxc5 ♘xc4 18 c6 ♘xa3! 19 cxd7+ ♕xd7 20 ♕xa3 ♕e7 21 ♕a4+ ♕d7 22 ♕a3 [preventing kingside castling], which leads to a draw by repetition after 22...♕e7) 22...0-0 17 ♗xd7 ♕xd7 18 ♘e5 ♕c7 19 a6!, breaking up the queenside with an advantage.

Instead 15...a6 (preventing a5-a6) is best, when Hübner suggests 16 ♖e3 ♘d6 17 ♗xe6 0-0-0 18 ♗xd6 ♕xd6 19 ♗c4 and ♖b3 with a dangerous attack.

16 ♘e5 a6 17 ♖ac1 ♖d8 18 ♗xa6!!

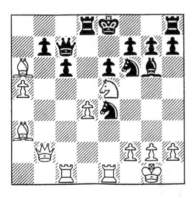

18...bxa6 19 ♘xc6 ♘g4 20 ♘e5! ♕xa5 21 ♘xg4 ♕b5 22 ♕c2?!

This is White's first inaccuracy in this fascinating game! Hübner notes that the simple 22 ♕xb5 axb5 23 ♖c7 ♖a8 24 ♗b4 ♖a4 25 ♖c8+ ♔d7 26 ♖xh8 ♖xb4 27 ♘e5 ♔c7 28 ♖c1+ ♔b7 29 f3 ♘f6 30 ♘xg6 would have been clearly better for White. The game now becomes a little random, due to mutual time pressure, but White pulls through in the end.

22...♘d6 23 ♕c7 ♖d7 24 ♕c3 0-0 25 ♘e5 ♖dd8 26 ♕c6? ♕xc6 27 ♖xc6 ♘b5 28 ♗xf8 ♔xf8 29 ♖xa6 ♘xd4 30 f3 f6?! 31 ♘xg6+ hxg6 32 f4 ♖d5 33 ♖e4 g5 34 ♖a4 e5 35 fxe5 fxe5 36 ♖a7 ♔g8 37 ♖e7

Now White is winning again.

37...♘c6 38 ♖e6 ♖c5 39 ♖g6 ♔f7 40 ♖xg5 g6 41 h4 ♔f6 42 ♔h2 ♘e7 43 ♖a4 ♖c6 44 ♖g3 ♘f5 45 ♖f3 ♔g7 46 ♖e4 ♖e6 47 h5 ♘e7 48 hxg6 ♘xg6 49 ♔h3 ♘e7 50 ♔g3 ♘g6 51 ♖f5 ♖e7 52 ♔g4 ♖a7 53 ♔g5 ♘h8 54 ♖g4 ♘f7+ 55 ♔h5+ ♔f8 56 ♔g6 ♔e8 57 ♖h4 1-0

Summary

The alert reader will have noticed my profound mistrust of the line 8...♘bd7 9 ♕e2 ♗g6 10 e4 ♗xc3 11 bxc3 ♘xe4. I honestly cannot understand the attraction of these lines for Black. Therefore, if Black wishes to try to prevent e3-e4, then Kramnik's 8...0-0 9 ♕e2 ♗g6 is the line for you; Yusupov's plan of a quick ♘h4 is the most testing response.

1 d4 d5 2 c4 c6 3 ♘f3 ♘f6 4 ♘c3 dxc4 5 a4 ♗f5 6 e3 e6 7 ♗xc4 ♗b4 8 0-0

8...0-0
> 8...♘bd7 *(D)*
>> 9 ♘h4 ♗g6
>>> 10 ♗e2 - *game 4*
>>> 10 h3 - *game 5*
>> 9 ♕e2 ♗g6 (9...♗g4 - see next chapter) 10 e4 ♗xc3 (10...♗g6 - see next chapter) 11 bxc3 ♘xe4 12 ♗a3 ♕c7
>>> 13 ♖fe1 - *game 8*
>>> 13 ♖fc1 0-0-0 14 a5 *(D)*
>>>> 14...♘d6 - *game 6*
>>>> 14...♔b8 - *game 7*

9 ♕e2
> 9 ♘h4 - *game 3*

9...♗g6
> 9...♘bd7 - see next chapter

10 ♘e5 ♘bd7 11 ♘xg6 hxg6 12 ♖d1 *(D)*
> 12...♕e7 - *game 1*
> 12...♕a5 - *game 2*

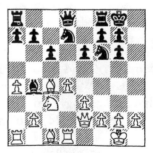

8...♘bd7

14 a5

12 ♖d1

CHAPTER TWO

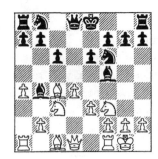

The Old Main Line: Black allows e3-e4

1 d4 d5 2 c4 c6 3 ♘f3 ♘f6 4 ♘c3 dxc4 5 a4 ♗f5 6 e3 e6 7 ♗xc4 ♗b4 8 0-0

This chapter deals with lines arising from 8...♘bd7 9 ♕e2 0-0 10 e4 ♗g6 (or 9...♗g6 10 e4 0-0, turning down the dangerous pawn sacrifice on the way) and 9...♗g4.

Question 1: When White plays e3-e4, he gains a commanding central presence with pawns on e4 and d4. Why is Black playing this position? Isn't he just worse?

Answer: Central pawns are strong if they are dynamic and able to advance and chase away the opposing pieces. Otherwise, they can present easy targets for the enemy pieces. In this case, White cannot advance d4-d5, and e4-e5 leaves a hole on d5 for the black pieces. Moreover, Black is threatening to win a pawn with ...♗xc3 and ♘xe4, now that his king is safely castled. Therefore, while the d4-e4 centre gives White a definite space advantage, Black has plenty of threats against the white centre, which is the basis of his counterplay.

Question 2: What is the difference between playing 9...♗g6 first or 9...0-0 10 e4 ♗g6?

Answer: Good question! Generally, black players play 9...♗g6 to pretend that they are willing to take on the pawn sacrifice after 10 e4. Even if they don't intend to take the pawn, the idea is to make White waste a little time on the clock thinking about his variations! You never know - a few minutes might be handy later!

Game 9
Gofshtein-Sadler
Ischia 1996

1 d4 d5 2 c4 c6 3 ♘f3 ♘f6 4 ♘c3 dxc4 5 a4 ♗f5 6 e3 e6 7 ♗xc4 ♗b4 8 0-0 ♘bd7 9 ♕e2 0-0 10 e4 ♗g6 11 ♗d3

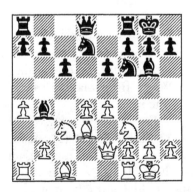

White had to deal with the threat

of ...♝xc3 and ...♞xe4. It is a general rule that the longer you can delay committing your centre, the better, since the later you reveal your hand, the less time your opponent has to adjust to it.

11...♝h5

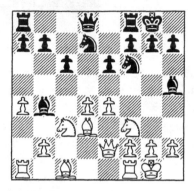

Question 3: What is the point of this move?

Answer: The first place to look for counterplay, is with your pawn breaks. Pawn breaks have two functions:

a) They attack the opponent's pawn structure and force him to react to you.

b) They are a 'breakout': they gain space and therefore give more room for your pieces to become active.

Black has two pawn breaks in this position: ...e6-e5 and ...c6-c5. Usually he prefers to aim for ...e6-e5, since this stops White from playing e4-e5 himself, inconveniencing the black knight. For example, 11...c5 12 e5! ♞d5 13 ♞xd5 exd5 (13...♝xd3 14 ♛xd3 exd5 15 ♞g5! is unpleasant) 14 ♝xg6 hxg6 15 ♞g5, with threats of e5-and ♛g4-h4 and ♛h7 mate, is nasty for Black. The move in the game pins

the knight on f3 to the queen and thus threatens ...e6-e5. The alternative 11...h6 is considered in Game 12.

12 ♝f4

Trying to avoid e4-e5 for a while longer, White brings another piece to bear on e5. Strangely enough, this is probably not the best move. The direct 12 e5 is considered in the next game.

12...♛e7!?

Black threatens 13...♝xf3 14 ♛xf3 e5!, equalising comfortably. I think that this is a novelty: 12...♖e8 had been played before.

13 e5

Absolutely necessary.

13...♞d5 14 ♞xd5 cxd5

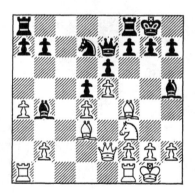

White has a space advantage due to his pawns on d4 and e5. Normally, with his bishops, knight and queen pointing towards the black king, White could consider launching a kingside attack, but here Black's bishop on h5 interferes with this plan: it can exchange itself for the knight on f3 or return to g6 to block any white attack on the b1-h7 diagonal.

Meanwhile Black will challenge for the c-file, exchanging the bishop on d3 for the one on g6 in order to free c2 as an entry square for the black major pieces. Black will also transfer his knight to c6 via b8 from where it not only attacks d4, but can invade the white queenside by a5-b3 or via b4. So what on earth can White do?

Stay calm! White does not want to exchange pieces on the c-file since this would help Black to free his cramped position, so he has two plans. First (my own favourite), he can concentrate on the kingside where White holds most of the trumps: a space advantage and a large concentration of minor pieces. I would try to push my kingside pawns: 15 h3 ♖fc8 16 g4 ♗g6 17 h4, intending h4-h5. This plan demonstrates the drawback to ♗f4, however: White would like to throw the f-pawn forward as well, but the bishop gets in the way. The chances after 15 h3 are, I believe, about equal. White's choice is interesting, but there is always a danger in choosing plans based mainly on tactical points: if there is just a little hole in your calculations, then you often find that you have just wasted time and must retreat in disarray. On the other hand, such plans are often the most unexpected and the most difficult for the opponent to deal with!

15 ♕e3 ♖fc8 16 a5!? ♗g6 17 ♖a4!?

At first I thought about playing 17...♖ab8, intending 18...b5 to drive away the white rook. Then to my horror I noticed 18 ♗b5! White is threatening to take the knight on d7 and then take my bishop on b4, so 18...♘f8 is natural, but then 19 ♕b3! and my bishop is trapped!

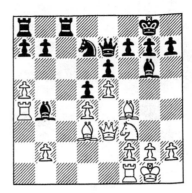

17...♗xd3 18 ♕xd3 ♖c4!

Black is now planning ...b7-b5 and 19 b3 is met by 19...♖c7!, when 20 ♕b5 does not win a piece as Black has 20...♗c3, when he stands well. Realising that his activity on the queenside has come to naught, White goes back to 'Plan A' and expands on the kingside, but he is several tempi down on what he could have had earlier.

19 h4 h6 20 h5 ♘c5!

Oops! My opponent had missed that one. However, after a big think, he came up with an active defence.

21 dxc5 ♖xf4 22 a6! bxa6 23 c6 a5 24 ♖c1 ♖c8 25 b3 ♖c7 26 ♖c2 ♖e4?!

A rather casual move. 26...♖f5 27

罝a1 罝xh5 28 g4 罝h3 29 ♔g2 ♕h4!! (this lovely move was pointed out to me by Julian Hodgson after the game) was the way to play.

27 罝a1 ♗c5?! 28 罝xa5 罝xc6??

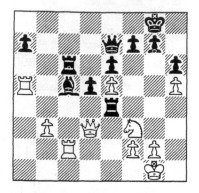

29 罝b5??

My God! I had missed that White could simply win a piece with 29 ♕b5, forking rook and bishop. I had thought that I could play 29...♗xf2+ with a discovered attack on the rook on c2, but White just plays 30 罝xf2! Luckily White shared the same blind spot! After 29 罝b5, White is just lost.

29...♕c7 30 罝a2 ♗b6

Trapping the rook.

31 ♔h2 罝c3 32 ♕d2 ♕c6 33 罝xb6 axb6 34 ♘d4 罝h4+ 0-1

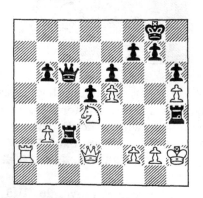

35 ♔g1 罝c1+ leads to immediate mate.

So 12 ♗f4 doesn't seem all that promising for White. What about 12 e5 instead?

> ### Game 10
> **Gelfand-Lautier**
> *Zurich 1994*

1 d4 d5 2 c4 c6 3 ♘f3 ♘f6 4 ♘c3 dxc4 5 a4 ♗f5 6 e3 e6 7 ♗xc4 ♗b4 8 0-0 ♘bd7 9 ♕e2 ♗g6 10 e4 0-0 11 ♗d3 ♗h5 12 e5

Probably the best move.

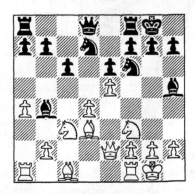

12...♘d5 13 ♘xd5

The alternative, 13 ♘e4, is dealt with in the next game.

13...cxd5

13...exd5 has been suggested, but since White already has a space advantage on the kingside, I am sceptical about conceding a pawn majority as well in that area.

14 ♕e3 h6?!

A debatable decision. I would prefer 14...♗e7, followed by a rook to the c-file and ...♘b8-c6.

15 ♘e1!

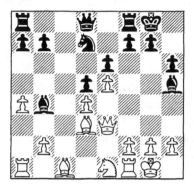

A very instructive plan: White intends to play f2-f4 and f4-f5, which is particularly dangerous once Black has weakened his kingside with ...h7-h6. Moreover, the knight will eventually come to d3 with tempo, hitting the bishop on b4.

15...f5 16 exf6 ♕xf6 17 ♗b5 ♘b8 18 ♘d3! a6

18...♗d6 19 ♘e5 is not pleasant for Black.

19 ♘xb4 axb5 20 a5 ♘a6 21 ♘d3! ♖fc8 22 ♗d2 ♖c2 23 ♖ac1 ♖ac8 24 ♖xc2 ♖xc2 25 ♖c1 ♖xc1+ 26 ♗xc1 ♗g6 27 ♘e5 ♕f5 28 h3 ♕c2 29 ♘xg6!

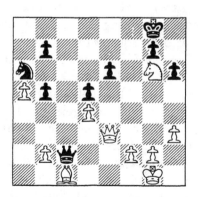

Excellent judgement. In the resulting position, White's bishop com-

pletely dominates the black knight.

29...♕xg6 30 ♕c3 ♔h7 31 ♗f4 ♕f7 32 ♗e5 ♕d7 33 h4 ♔g8 34 h5!

Fixing the g7-pawn.

34...♕d8 35 ♕g3 ♕d7 36 ♗d6 ♕f7 37 ♕e5 ♕f5 38 ♕e2 b4 39 g4 ♕f6 40 ♗e5 ♕g5 41 ♔g2 b3 42 ♗d6!

Preventing the knight from becoming active.

42...♔f7 43 ♕d1 ♔g8 44 ♗g3 ♕f6 45 ♗e5 ♕h4 46 ♗g3 ♕f6 47 ♕d2 ♕e7 48 ♕e3 ♕f6 49 ♗d6 ♔h7 50 ♕xb3 ♕xd4 51 ♕c2+ ♔h8 52 ♕c8+ ♔h7 53 ♕c2+ ♔h8 54 ♕c8+ ♔h7 55 ♕xe6!

Protecting g4.

55...♕xb2 56 ♗e5 ♕c2 57 ♕e7 ♕e4+ 58 ♔g3 ♕d3+ 1-0

After 59 f3, Black cannot stop mate. His knight has not moved since move 20!

Black should be fine after the exchange of knights on d5, providing he avoids weakening his kingside. Let us take a look at 13 ♘e4.

Game 11
Xu Jun-Akopian
Moscow Olympiad 1994

---

1 d4 d5 2 c4 c6 3 ♘f3 ♘f6 4 ♘c3 dxc4 5 a4 ♗f5 6 e3 e6 7 ♗xc4 ♗b4 8 0-0 ♘bd7 9 ♕e2 ♗g6 10 e4 0-0 11 ♗d3 ♗h5 12 e5 ♘d5 13 ♘e4!?

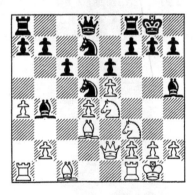

Many white players do not enjoy the positions that we have seen in the first two games of this chapter. With the centre closed, and the prospect of exchanges on the c-file, they feel uneasy about their winning prospects; so recently the plan with 13 ♘e4 has come to prominence. Of course, Black keeps his knight outpost on d5 and his pawn-break against the centre with ...c6-c5. However, White's space advantage remains and he retains e4 to transfer first his knight, then his queen to the kingside. Yes, this is the hacker's option!

13...♗e7

13...c5 is unpleasantly met by 14 ♗g5! ♕a5 15 ♗b5! Once Black moves the knight on d7, he will lose the c5-pawn, and he cannot protect it with a rook due to the bishop on g5. If he protects the knight with 15...♕c7, then 16 ♖ac1 is unpleasant. The text prevents ♗g5 and prepares ...c6-c5.

14 ♘g3

The direct approach. 14 a5 has also been tried.

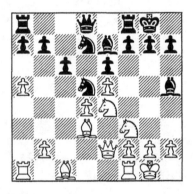

Question 4: Why does White play 14 a5?

Answer: a4-a5 gains queenside space, preventing Black from using the a5 or b6 squares for his pieces.

Question 5: So what's the verdict? Is it a good move?

Answer: Absolutely not! These aims are completely irrelevant. 14...c5 is logical, striking at the d4-pawn. Neither 15 dxc5 ♘xe5 nor 15 ♘xc5 ♘xc5 (15...♗xc5!?) 16 dxc5 ♖c8 (of course not 16...♗xc5 17 ♗xh7+ ♔xh7 18 ♕c2+ ♔g8 19 ♘g5 ♗g6 20 ♕xc5, winning a pawn), followed by ...♗xc5 or ...♖xc5, promise White anything.

14...♗g6

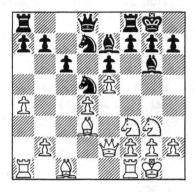

15 ♗xg6 hxg6

15...fxg6 used to be played almost automatically, primarily for defensive reasons: black players were worried that if they recaptured with the h-pawn, White would play his knight on g3 to g5 via e4 and his queen to h4, when Black would have no defence to ♕h7 mate. By taking with the f-pawn Black retains the option of...h7-h6 to keep a knight out of g5, and of course, he gains the semi-open f-file for counterplay. And then people realised that White's attack was hardly automatic after 15...hxg6, so this move gradually became the main line!

16 ♘e4 c5

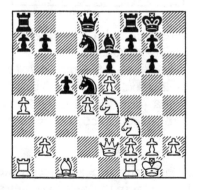

17 ♘c3

This is a perfectly reasonable plan, challenging Black's knight on d5 once Black has weakened its support by playing ...c6-c5, but why did the Chinese player avoid 17 ♘eg5? 17...cxd4 18 ♕e4 ♖e8 19 ♕h4 ♘f8 seems to be a good reason. The knight on f8 defends against ♕h7 and if by some miracle White manages to threaten to get a rook on h3, then Black can hit the 'panic button' and chase the knight away with ...f7-f6. White could, however, try and open up the black kingside with h2-h4-h5, possibly after 16 ♕e4 c5 17 h4 cxd4 18 h5!? And now it's up to *you*, the reader! We'll have to wait for practical tests before a conclusion can be reached.

17...♕b6

17...♘7b6 18 a5 ♘xc3 19 bxc3 ♘d5 20 c4 ♘b4 also seems reasonable.

18 ♘xd5 exd5 19 dxc5 ♘xc5 20 ♗e3 ♕e6 21 a5 a6 22 ♖ac1 ♖ac8 23 ♖fd1 ♘b3 24 ♖xc8 ♖xc8

Black has an isolated d-pawn, but White's queenside is weak. The position is about equal.

25 ♗b6 ♗d8?! 26 ♗xd8 ♖xd8 27 ♕e1?!

Black's slightly incautious 25th move allowed White the chance to activate his queen by the lovely 27 ♕e4!, intending ♘g5 and ♕h4, as 27...dxe4 allows 28 ♖xd8+ ♔h7 29 ♘g5+ winning the queen (analysis by Xu Jun). The rest is hard-fought, but it was always going to be a draw.

27...♕e7 28 ♕c3 ♘c5 29 ♕b4 ♔f8 30 ♔f1 ♘e6 31 ♕xe7+ ♔xe7 32 ♖d3 d4 33 ♖b3 ♖d7 34 g3 ♘d8 35 ♖b6 ♖d5 36 b4 d3 37 ♔e1 ♔d7 38 ♔d2 ♔c7 39 ♖d6 ♖xd6 40 exd6+ ♔xd6 41 ♔xd3 ♔d5 42 ♘d2 ♘c6 43 ♔c3 ♘e5 44 ♘b3 ♘c4 45 f4 f6 ½-½

Game 12
I.Sokolov-Oll
Moscow Olympiad 1994

---

1 d4 d5 2 c4 c6 3 ♘c3 ♘f6 4 ♘f3 dxc4 5 a4 ♗f5 6 e3 e6 7 ♗xc4 ♗b4 8 0-0 ♘bd7 9 ♕e2 ♗g6 10 e4 0-0 11 ♗d3 h6

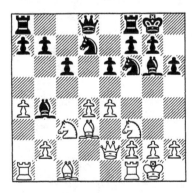

So far, we have only examined the direct 11...♗h5. Here Black develops quietly and waits for an opportunity to break with either ...c6-c5 or ...e6-e5. This is a slightly risky approach as

you can really get sat on if you are not careful, but the following game is a nice illustration of a typical struggle. White always enjoys a slight pull, but Black patiently neutralises his initiative.

11...♕a5 has a similar idea. After 12 ♗f4! ♖fe8 (12...♗xc3 13 bxc3 ♕xc3 loses to 14 ♗d2 ♕c2 15 ♗d3 ♕b2 16 ♖fb1) 13 h3 ♖ac8 14 ♘a2!, White had a slight advantage in Beliavsky-Short, Linares 1995, as 14...♗f8 (14...♕xa4 15 ♘c3! ♕b3 16 ♗c4 wins the queen) 15 b4! gains queenside space with tempo: 15...♕xa4 16 ♖fb1 and ♘a2-c3 traps the queen, while 15...♗xb4 16 ♘xb4 ♕xb4 17 ♖fb1 ♕a5 18 ♖xb7 is unpleasant for Black.

12 ♗f4 ♖c8 13 h3 ♖e8 14 ♖fd1 a6 15 ♘a2 ♗f8 16 b4 a5!

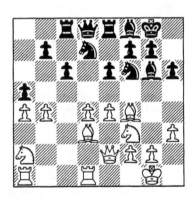

A very good idea, breaking White's grip on the c5-square.

17 bxa5 ♕xa5 18 ♗d2 ♕c7 19 e5 ♗xd3 20 ♕xd3 ♘d5 21 ♘c3 ♘xc3 22 ♗xc3 ♘b6 23 a5 ♘d5 24 ♗e1 c5! 25 dxc5 ♗xc5 26 ♕b5 ♕c6 ½-½

Occasionally 9...♗g4 is seen instead of 9...♗g6, as in the next two games.

Game 13
Khalifman-Kir.Georgiev
Elenite 1994

1 d4 d5 2 ♘f3 ♘f6 3 c4 dxc4 4
♘c3 c6 5 a4 ♗f5 6 e3 e6 7 ♗xc4
♗b4 8 0-0 ♘bd7 9 ♕e2 ♗g4!?

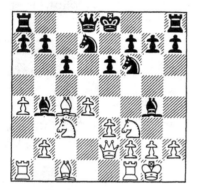

A rather unusual move that aims to
bore White to tears by exchanging off
into a dull ending.
**10 ♖d1 ♕a5! 11 e4 ♕h5 12 h3
♗xf3 13 ♕xf3 ♕xf3 14 gxf3 0-0 15
a5**

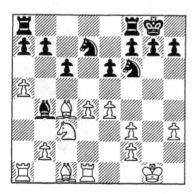

White has the two bishops and a
space advantage, but Black is extremely solid and has no pawn weaknesses.

**15...a6 16 ♗e2 ♖fd8 17 ♖a4 ♗e7
18 f4 ♘e8 19 ♗e3 ♖ac8 20 ♗f3
♘d6 21 ♗e2 g6 22 ♖aa1 ½-½**

Here Kasparov shows a more critical approach for White.

Game 14
Kasparov-Bareev
Novgorod 1994

1 d4 d5 2 c4 c6 3 ♘f3 ♘f6 4 ♘c3
dxc4 5 a4 ♗f5 6 e3 e6 7 ♗xc4 ♗b4
8 0-0 ♘bd7 9 ♕e2 ♗g4 10 h3!

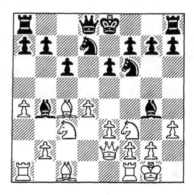

The most aggressive idea: now if
10...♗h5, White can play for e3-e4
without fear of the ...♕a5-h5 manoeuvre.
**10...♗xf3 11 ♕xf3 0-0 12 ♖d1 ♕a5
13 e4 e5 14 d5**
This bears a distinct similarity to
Richardson-Sadler from Chapter 1.
White's queen is better placed on f3
than e2, though of course Black's
queen is more actively placed as well.
**14...♘b6 15 ♗b3 ♗xc3 16 bxc3
cxd5 17 exd5 ♖ac8 18 c4!!**
Brilliant. 18...♘xc4 19 ♗g5 ♕a6 20
d6! ♘xd6 21 ♗xf6 gxf6 22 ♕xf6 ♘c4
23 ♕xa6 bxa6 24 ♖d7 is clearly better

for White (Kasparov).

18...♖fe8 19 ♗d2 ♕a6 20 d6! ♘bd7 21 ♗e3 ♖c6 22 a5! ♖xd6 23 ♗a4 ♖xd1+ 24 ♖xd1 ♖d8 25 c5!

Black has been tied up in quite brilliant fashion.

25...h6 26 ♕f5 g6 27 ♕c2! ♕xa5 28 ♖d6 ♔g7 29 ♕d1 ♕c7 30 h4 ♔h8 31 h5 g5 32 ♕f3 ♔g7 33 ♕f5

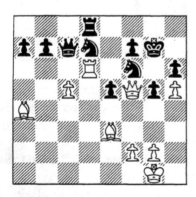

33...b6 34 ♗xd7! ♘xd7 35 ♗xg5! 1-0

Kasparov gives 35...hxg5 36 ♕xg5 ♔f8 37 h6 bxc5 38 h7 winning. A really magical game.

Question 6: In your own games you have played both 8...0-0 and 8...♘bd7. Which is the better move?

Answer: I can offer no definitive conclusion: in theory, 8...0-0 and 8...♘bd7 are equally good. However, practical chess is not only about finding the very best move: when making a final decision whether to play 8...0-0 or 8...♘bd7, it is also necessary to take the strength of your opponent into account. The following game shows why.

> ### Game 15
> ### D.Strauss-Lakdawala
> *USA 1992*

1 d4 d5 2 c4 c6 3 ♘f3 ♘f6 4 ♘c3 dxc4 5 a4 ♗f5 6 e3 e6 7 ♗xc4 ♗b4 8 0-0 ♘bd7 9 ♕b3

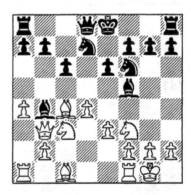

This move forces a draw by repetition if White desires after 9...a5 (best) 10 ♘a2 (chasing the bishop away) 10...♗e7 11 ♕xb7 ♖b8 12 ♕a6 (12 ♕xc6 ♖b6!) 12...♖a8 13 ♕xc6 ♖c8 14 ♕b5 ♖b8, as the queen cannot escape from the rook's attack. So if your opponent is much weaker than you, or you desperately need a win, you must play 8...0-0, as 9 ♕b3 ♕e7! (protecting b7 and facilitating ...c6-c5) is nothing for White. Alert readers will observe that I chose 8...0-0 against Richardson in just such a must-win situation. The attempt to avoid the repetition in this game is brutally dealt with.

9...♛b6 10 e4

10...♝g6

10...♞xe4 11 ♞xe4 ♝xe4 12 ♝xe6! is clearly better for White.

11 ♝xe6! fxe6 12 a5!

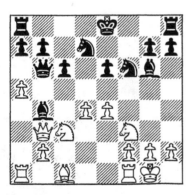

Diverting the bishop to an inferior square.

12...♝xa5 13 ♛xe6+ ♚d8 14 e5 ♞e4 15 ♞xe4! ♝xe4 16 ♛f7!!

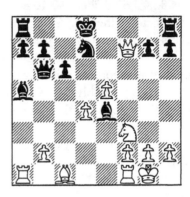

A brilliant discovery of David Gliksman. The queen moves to allow the e-pawn to advance.

16...♜f8

The situation is already desperate. 16...♝xf3 17 e6! (D.Strauss) 17...♞f6 18 e7+ ♚c8 19 ♛e6+ ♚c7 (19...♞d7 20 e8♛) 20 ♝f4+ wins, while instead 16...♝g6 17 ♛xg7 ♜e8 18 d5!! (again D.Strauss), opening more central lines, is crushing as 18...cxd5 19 ♝g5+ ♚c8 20 ♜fc1+ is appalling for Black.

17 ♛xg7 ♝d5 18 e6! ♝xe6 19 ♛g5+!

Now the point of 12 a5 is revealed: this check picks up the bishop!

19...♚c8 20 ♜xa5 ♜g8 21 ♛h5 ♝g4 22 ♜g5! ♝xh5 23 ♜xg8+ ♞f8 24 ♜xf8+ ♚d7 25 ♞e5+ ♚c7 26 ♜xa8 ♛xd4 27 ♜e1 ♝e2 28 ♜e8 c5 29 ♜e7+ ♚c8 30 ♞c6 1-0

Summary

After 8...♘bd7 9 ♕e2 0-0 10 e4 ♗g6 11 ♗d3 ♗h5, 12 e5 is probably White's best try and after 12...♘d5, hackers should choose 13 ♘e4 and positional players should favour 13 ♘xd5 and 14 ♕e3. These positions are complicated and interesting in all cases. After Kasparov's brutal treatment, 9...♗g4 should probably be avoided unless you spot a flaw in 'Gazza's' analysis. If you do, then you're probably Mr Karpov! But remember, if you desperately need a win as Black, 8...0-0 is the only way to play.

1 d4 d5 2 c4 c6 3 ♘f3 ♘f6 4 ♘c3 dxc4 5 a4 ♗f5 6 e3 e6 7 ♗xc4 ♗b4 8 0-0

8...0-0

      8...♘bd7 *(D)*

            9 ♕e2 ♗g4

                 10 ♖d1 - *game 13*

                 10 h3 - *game 14*

            9 ♕b3 - *game 15*

9 ♕e2 ♘bd7 10 e4 ♗g6 11 ♗d3 ♗h5 *(D)*

      11...h6 - *game 12*

12 e5

      12 ♗f4 - *game 9*

12...♘d5 *(D)*

      13 ♘xd5 - *game 10*

      13 ♘e4 - *game 11*

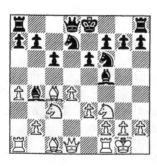

    8...♘bd7   *11...♗h5*   *12...♘d5*

CHAPTER THREE

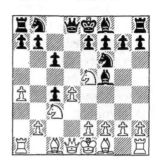

The New Main Line:
Black fights for control of e4

1 d4 d5 2 c4 c6 3 ♘f3 ♘f6 4 ♘c3 dxc4 5 a4 ♗f5 6 ♘e5

The sequence 1 d4 d5 2 c4 c6 3 ♘f3 ♘f6 4 ♘c3 dxc4 5 a4 ♗f5 6 ♘e5 is the latest fashion at the highest level. 6 ♘e5 truly is a 'modern' move: White does not worry about putting his king into safety; he tries immediately to achieve e2-e4 by moving the knight to e5 and playing f2-f3. In principle Black should not allow White to achieve e2-e4, since here it is ideally defended by a pawn on f3, leaving the white pieces free for active operations. In this chapter, Black continues the fight for e4 with an interesting piece sacrifice:

6...e6 7 f3 ♗b4

Pinning the knight on c3 and thus fighting for e4.

8 e4

...and after this there is no going back!

8...♗xe4 9 fxe4 ♘xe4 10 ♗d2

10 ♕f3 leads to a well-known draw by repetition after 10...♕xd4 11 ♕xf7+ ♔d8 12 ♗g5+! ♘xg5 13 ♕xg7 ♗xc3+ 14 bxc3 ♕xc3+ 15 ♔e2 ♕c2+ 16 ♔e1 ♕c3+, etc.

10...♕xd4 11 ♘xe4 ♕xe4+ 12 ♕e2 ♗xd2+ 13 ♔xd2 ♕d5+

Question 1: What is the material balance?

Answer: Black has four pawns for a piece, though it is touch and go whether he can hang on to the c4-pawn. Even three pawns, however, is good material compensation for the temporarily rather inactive bishop on f1.

> ### Game 16
> ### Lalic-Sadler
> *Hastings 1995/96*

1 c4 c6 2 d4 d5 3 ♘f3 ♘f6 4 ♘c3 dxc4 5 a4 ♗f5 6 ♘e5 e6 7 f3 ♗b4 8 e4 ♗xe4 9 fxe4 ♘xe4 10 ♗d2 ♕xd4 11 ♘xe4 ♕xe4+ 12 ♕e2 ♗xd2+ 13 ♔xd2 ♕d5+ 14 ♔c3

After 14 ♔c2 ♘a6, which is considered in the next game, White always has to worry about ...♘a6-b4+, which can be irritating. Therefore white players began to experiment with 14 ♔c3, avoiding this sort of counterplay. The one drawback to the king on c3, however, is that it is just within reach of the black queenside pawns, so Black can play an aggressive continuation that would not succeed against 14 ♔c2.

14...0-0! 15 ♕e3

This looks incomprehensible - what is wrong with 15 ♘xc4? The problem is 15...b5! 16 ♘e5 and now 16...b4+! The king's exposed placement gives Black a vital extra tempo for the attack. 17 ♔xb4 is met by 17...♘a6+! 18 ♔a3 (18 ♕xa6 ♖ab8+! 19 ♔c3 ♕xe5+ winning) 18...♖ab8 19 ♕e3 ♕d6+ 20 ♔a2 ♘b4+ 21 ♔b1 ♕d1+ 22 ♕c1 ♕d4! (threatening ...♕xe5 and ...♕e4+) 23 ♕e1 ♘c2!

---
see following diagram

Thanks to this powerful knight thrust, Black is now winning by force. Fasten your seat belts, a rather long variation lies ahead!

24 ♔xc2 ♕xb2+ 25 ♔d3 ♖b3+ 26 ♔e4 f5+ 27 ♔f4 ♕d4+ 28 ♔g5 ♕d8+ 29 ♔h5 ♕e8+ 30 ♔h4 ♕e7+ 31 ♔h5 g6+ 32 ♔h6 ♕g7+ 33 ♔g5 h6+ 34 ♔f4 g5 mate!

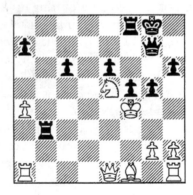

The attempt to turn down the gift with 17 ♔c2 is met by 17...b3+ 18 ♔c3 ♘a6! 19 ♕e3 (19 ♕xa6 ♕xe5+ 20 ♔xb3 ♖ab8+ wins for Black) 19...♖ab8 (intending ...♘b4) 19 ♗xa6 ♕a5+ 20 ♔d3 ♕xa6+ 21 ♔e4 with a crazy position, where anything could happen (especially to the white king!).

15 ♕e3 first of all aims to take control of some dark squares; secondly, White frees the bishop to develop and threatens ♗xc4.

15...b5! 16 ♗e2

Instead 16 axb5 cxb5 17 ♗e2 ♘d7! 18 ♘xd7 ♕xd7 19 ♗f3 ♖ac8 20 ♖xa7 b4+! 21 ♔c2 (Hübner points out that 21 ♔xb4 loses to 21...♖b8+ 22 ♔a3 ♕d6+ 23 ♔a2 ♖b3 24 ♕f2 ♖fb8) 21...♕b5 gave White nothing in the stem game Gelfand-Hübner, Munich 1992. Even if White wins both of the black queenside pawns for his b-pawn, and manages to swap off the queens and both sets of rooks, the resulting ending is likely to be drawn since White has the wrong-coloured rook's pawn for his bishop. Hence, all Black needs to do is to aim for a position like

and he will draw since the best White can achieve is

which is stalemate! The game continued 22 ♖d1 b3+ 23 ♔b1 g6 24 g4 (taking f5 from the black queen) 24...♕b8 25 ♖a4, when 25...♕b5 26 ♖a7 ♕b8 would have led to a draw by repetition according to Hübner, while 25...♕xh2!? 26 ♖c1 c3 27 bxc3 ♖fd8 led to great complications.

16...♘d7 17 ♘xd7 ♕xd7 18 ♕c5

A new idea. Piket had earlier played 18 ♗f3 against Kramnik, but Black's strategy is similar in both cases.

18...a6! 19 ♖hd1 ½-½

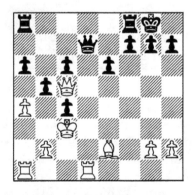

Exciting stuff, this grandmaster chess! 18...a6! was in fact a strong new idea and showed (I think) good understanding of the position. Black has four pawns for the piece, which is ample. However, his pieces are passive and he has to find a way to activate them. White is strong on the light squares (he has a light-squared bishop), but weak on the dark squares, so I have to put my queen in contact with some dark squares. The c7-square is the obvious spot since from there the queen eyes a5, e5, f4 and the h2-pawn. However, I obviously couldn't play 18...♕c7, as 19 axb5 would win for White. Therefore 18...a6! seemed logical, and after a little calculation I saw that it was indeed the best move. For example, after 19...♕c7, 20 ♖d6? ♖ad8! 21 ♖xc6 ♕f4! is extremely worrying for White.

The next game is intended as a cautionary tale for black players, and I hope that my opponent will forgive me for using it in this way. Cynics may point out that I am demonstrating one of my rare wins from a catastrophic British Championship!

> ### Game 17
> ### Sadler-Ferguson
> *British Championship 1996*

1 d4 d5 2 c4 c6 3 ♘f3 ♘f6 4 ♘c3 dxc4 5 a4 ♗f5 6 ♘e5 e6 7 f3 ♗b4 8 e4 ♗xe4 9 fxe4 ♘xe4 10 ♗d2 ♕xd4 11 ♘xe4 ♕xe4+ 12 ♕e2 ♗xd2+ 13 ♔xd2 ♕d5+ 14 ♔c2 ♘a6

Black cannot hold on to the c4-pawn with 14...b5 as 15 ♖d1 ♕c5 16 axb5 axb5 17 ♕f3!, attacking f7 and the rook on a8, is just one way of exploiting Black's mistake.

15 ♘xc4 0-0-0 16 ♕e3 ♔b8

The more active alternative, 16...♘c5, is considered in Game 22.

17 ♗e2

17...♕xg2 wins a pawn, but after 18 ♖hg1 ♕xh2 19 ♖xg7 he has problems defending his second rank.

17...♔a8 18 g4!

Black has played rather slowly, putting his king to safety in the corner, so White begins to take control. This nice move takes away the annoying check on f5 from the black queen.

18...♕d7

A novelty. Kramnik-Kir.Georgiev, Moscow Olympiad 1994, had continued 18...f6 19 ♖hd1 ♕g2 20 ♖xd8 ♖xd8 21 ♕xe6 with a clear advantage for White.

19 ♖ad1 ♘b4+ 20 ♔b1 ♘d5

Black has got his knight to a central outpost on d5, but it is hard to suggest another active thing for him to do.

21 ♕a3 ♕c7 22 a5 ♔b8 23 a6!

Softening up the black queenside.

23...b6 24 ♗f3 ♖he8 25 ♖he1 f6 26 ♕b3 ♔a8 27 h4! b5 28 ♘e3 ♕a5

A desperate attempt to break out, but one that is easily refuted.

29 ♘xd5 exd5 30 ♖xe8 ♖xe8 31 ♖xd5!

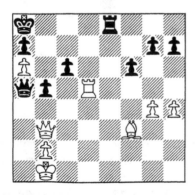

31...♔b8

31...exd5 is met by 32 ♕xd5+ and mates.

32 ♖d6 ♕xa6 33 ♗xc6 ♖e1+ 34 ♔c2 ♔c7 35 ♖d7+ ♔b6 36 ♗xb5 1-0

Question 2: What went wrong? Why did Black lose without seemingly being able to put up any sort of fight?

Answer: Black knew very little about this line and was extremely unfortunate that this is one of those variations where knowledge is essential: the big decisions for Black are strategical - there is almost no chance to calculate your way out of trouble. Black must understand where and when to exchange queens; where to aim to put his knight; and how to arrange his pawns. Without this knowledge, Black has little chance of success.

Question 3: How does one acquire this knowledge?

Answer: One must study games in this line and draw conclusions from them.

Game 18
Kramnik-Lautier
Linares 1994

---

1 ♘f3 d5 2 d4 ♘f6 3 c4 c6 4 ♘c3 dxc4 5 a4 ♗f5 6 ♘e5 e6 7 f3 ♗b4 8 e4 ♗xe4 9 fxe4 ♘xe4 10 ♗d2 ♕xd4 11 ♘xe4 ♕xe4+ 12 ♕e2 ♗xd2+ 13 ♔xd2 ♕d5+ 14 ♔c2 ♘a6 15 ♘xc4 0-0-0

Black has castled queenside, and not kingside. Why? First, castling queenside brings a rook immediately to the open d-file; second, if White exchanges queens, the black king is well-placed to protect the queenside pawns from a potential attack by the white knight.

16 ♕e5 f6 17 ♕xd5

The more critical 17 ♕e3 is discussed in Games 20 and 21.

17...cxd5

Here Black has exchanged queens on his own terms: he has forced White to take on d5. We can conclude that the exchange of queens is only acceptable to Black if it improves the black pawn structure. Also, Black should recapture on d5 with the c-pawn: after ...e6xd5, Black has just a 4-2 majority on the queenside; after ...c6xd5, Black has a pawn chain of five against just two white kingside pawns on g2 and h2. Black is more likely to be able to create passed pawns and a pawn chain that will restrict the white pieces with the latter rather than the former.

18 ♘a3 ♘b4+ 19 ♔d2 ♔d7 20 ♖c1 ♖c8 21 ♖c3 b6 22 ♗b5+ ♔d6 23 ♗e2 a6

Preventing ♘b5+.

24 h4 ♖hf8 25 h5 f5 26 h6

A typical attacking idea for White. Although White runs the risk of losing this pawn, as it is now cut off from the rest of its troops, if White can get a knight to g5 or a bishop to g8...

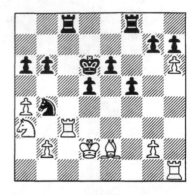

26...g6 27 ♖hc1 ♖c5 28 a5 ♘a2! 29 ♖xc5 bxc5 30 ♖a1 ♘b4 31 ♘c2 ♘c6 32 ♗xa6 ♖a8 33 ♗b5 ♖xa5 34 ♖xa5 ♘xa5 35 ♘e1 ♘b7 36 ♘f3 ♔e7 37 ♘g5 ♘d6 38 ♘xh7 ♘f7!

Just in time!

39 g4 ♘xh6 40 gxf5 gxf5 41 ♔e3 e5

Black's pawns are now very dangerous and White must play accurately.

42 ♗c6 ♔d6 43 ♗b7 ♘g4+ 44 ♔f3 e4+ 45 ♔f4 ♘e5 46 ♗a6 c4 47 ♘g5 ♘d3+ 48 ♔e3 f4+ 49 ♔d4 e3 50 ♘f3 e2 51 ♗b7 ♘e5 52 ♘e1 ♘d3 53 ♘f3 ♘e5 54 ♘e1 f3 55 ♔e3 ♔c5 56 ♔f2 ♔d4 57 ♘xf3+ ♘xf3 58 ♔xe2 ♘e5 59 ♔d2 ♘d3 60 ♗xd5

♔xd5 61 b3 ½-½

So what if White does not swap queens?

Game 19
Karpov-Hjartarson
Tilburg 1988

1 d4 d5 2 c4 c6 3 ♘f3 ♘f6 4 ♘c3 dxc4 5 a4 ♗f5 6 ♘e5 e6 7 f3 ♗b4 8 e4 ♗xe4 9 fxe4 ♘xe4 10 ♗d2 ♕xd4 11 ♘xe4 ♕xe4+ 12 ♕e2 ♗xd2+ 13 ♔xd2 ♕d5+ 14 ♔c2 ♘a6 15 ♘xc4 0-0-0 16 ♕e5 f6 17 ♕e3!?

At the time, this was a new idea. White is claiming that he has forced his opponent to weaken the pawn structure around his king.

17...c5!?

17...♔b8 is considered in the next two games.

18 ♔b3 ♘b4

Black's plan seems very logical: he is aiming to put a knight on d4.

19 ♖c1! ♘c6 20 ♔a3! ♘d4 21 ♘a5! e5 22 ♕c3! b6 23 ♘b3

This game is still the model for dealing with ...c6-c5 and ...♘b4. White weakens Black's light squares by forcing all his pawns to dark-squares, which makes it easy for White to blockade them with his bishop.

23...♕xb3+ 24 ♕xb3 ♘xb3 25 ♔xb3 ♖d4 26 h4! ♖hd8 27 ♗c4 ♔c7 28 h5 ♖g4 29 h6!

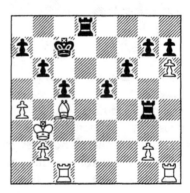

It's that plan again! Now the black kingside pawns are softened up and White gradually assumes complete control.

29...♖xg2 30 hxg7 ♖xg7 31 ♖cf1 ♖d6 32 ♖h6 e4 33 ♖hxf6 h5 34 ♖6f4 ♖d4 35 ♖f7+ ♖d7 36 ♖xg7 ♖xg7 37 ♖f4 ♖g3+ 38 ♔c2 ♖g2+ 39 ♔c3 ♖g3+ 40 ♔d2 ♖g4 41 ♖f7+ ♔d6 42 ♔e3 a6 1-0

A really impressive game from Karpov.

Game 20
Shirov-Bareev
Biel 1991

1 d4 d5 2 c4 ♘f6 3 ♘c3 c6 4 ♘f3
dxc4 5 a4 ♗f5 6 ♘e5 e6 7 f3 ♗b4
8 e4 ♗xe4 9 fxe4 ♘xe4 10 ♗d2
♕xd4 11 ♘xe4 ♕xe4+ 12 ♕e2
♗xd2+ 13 ♔xd2 ♕d5+ 14 ♔c2 ♘a6
15 ♘xc4 0-0-0 16 ♕e5 f6 17 ♕e3
♔b8 18 ♗e2 ♕xg2!?

Seeking to reduce White's winning
chances by exchanging as many
pawns as possible. The less greedy
18...e5 is considered in the next game.
19 ♖hg1 ♕xh2 20 ♖xg7 ♘b4+

Centralising the knight with tempi.

21 ♔b3 ♘d5 22 ♕f3 ♕f4 23 ♖f1
♕d4 24 ♕f2 ♕xf2 25 ♖xf2 ♔c8!

The key move, preparing ...♖d7 to
contest the second rank.
26 ♗g4 f5 27 ♗h5 ♖d7 28 ♖fg2
♖hd8 29 ♘e5 ♖xg7 30 ♖xg7 ♘f4
31 ♖xh7 ♖d5! 32 ♘g6 ♘xg6 33
♗xg6 ♖d7!

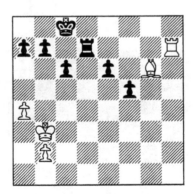

The ending is equal according to
Bareev.
34 ♔c4 ♖xh7 35 ♗xh7 ♔d7 36 ♔c5
b6+ 37 ♔c4 a5 38 ♗g6 ♔d6 39
♗e8 e5 40 ♗h5 e4 41 ♗e8 c5 42
♔c3 ♔e5 43 ♗d7 f4 44 ♗b5 f3 45
♗a6 ½-½

This is probably fine in general for
Black, but not very inspiring. I prefer

the more active plan that Black adopted in the next game.

Game 21
Kramnik-Ivanchuk
Linares 1994

1 ♘f3 d5 2 d4 ♘f6 3 c4 c6 4 ♘c3 dxc4 5 a4 ♗f5 6 ♘e5 e6 7 f3 ♗b4 8 e4 ♗xe4 9 fxe4 ♘xe4 10 ♗d2 ♕xd4 11 ♘xe4 ♕xe4+ 12 ♕e2 ♗xd2+ 13 ♔xd2 ♕d5+ 14 ♔c2 ♘a6 15 ♘xc4 0-0-0 16 ♕e5 f6 17 ♕e3 ♔b8! 18 ♗e2 e5!

This is the best set-up for Black: pawns on f6 and e5, keeping the queenside pawns where they are, while transferring pieces to the two outposts d4 and d5. Sometimes, Black will transfer the knight to d4 via c5 and e6.

19 g3 ♕e6 20 b3 ♖d5 21 ♔b2 ♖hd8 22 ♖ad1 ♘b4 23 ♕c3 ♕e7 24 ♘e3 ♖xd1 25 ♖xd1 ♖xd1 26 ♗xd1 g6 27 ♕d2 ♔c7 28 ♘c2 a5!

An important move, securing the knight on b4. If White could success- fully play a4-a5, then the knight could become vulnerable and Black would have to be careful.

29 ♘e3 ♕c5 30 ♘c4 b6 31 ♔b1 ½-½

Neither side has an obvious way to continue.

It is time to draw a few conclusions:
1. Black should castle queenside.
2. If the queens are to be ex-changed, Black wants them to be ex-changed on d5, when he will improve his pawn structure with ...c6xd5.
3. Black's ideal outpost for his knight is on d4 and not d5.
4. Black's best pawn structure in the middlegame is to place his pawns on a7, b7, c6, e5, f6, g7 and h7, since this creates two central outposts, d4 and d5.

But this is not the end of the story.

Game 22
Kramnik-Shirov
Dortmund 1996

1 ♘f3 d5 2 d4 c6 3 c4 ♘f6 4 ♘c3 dxc4 5 a4 ♗f5 6 ♘e5 e6 7 f3 ♗b4 8 e4 ♗xe4 9 fxe4 ♘xe4 10 ♗d2 ♕xd4 11 ♘xe4 ♕xe4+ 12 ♕e2 ♗xd2+ 13 ♔xd2 ♕d5+ 14 ♔c2 ♘a6 15 ♘xc4 0-0-0 16 ♕e3!

With hindsight, very obvious! This is the very latest idea in this line: White avoids giving Black the extra tempo ...f7-f6, forcing Black to look for another defensive formation.

16...♘c5 17 ♗e2 ♕xg2 18 ♖hg1 ♕xh2 19 ♖xg7!

This move was originally thought to be impossible due to 19...♖d3, but 20 ♖h1! is very strong for White after 20...♖xe3 21 ♖xh2 or 20...♕xh1 21 ♗xd3.

19...♖d4?!?

An amazing attempt that just falls short. When I started to analyse this position, I wanted to play 19...♖hg8, aiming to meet 20 ♖xf7 with 20...♖g2, but 21 ♕xc5 ♖xe2+ 22 ♔b3 ♖d3+ 23

♔a2 is just winning for White: his king is fact perfectly safe. 20...♖g5!? and 20...♕g2 (threatening ...♕g6+) are both interesting, but the onus is clearly on Black to find a reasonable continuation.

20 ♕xd4 ♕xe2+ 21 ♘d2 ♖d8 22 ♕c5 ♖xd2+ 23 ♔b3 ♖xb2+ 24 ♔a3

Amazingly White's king is quite safe, and now it is just a matter of the material telling in the end.

24...♖d2 25 ♖g3 ♕e4 26 ♖b3 b6 27 ♕f8+ ♔b7 28 ♕xf7+ ♔a6 29 ♕f3 ♕xf3 30 ♖xf3 ♔a5 31 ♖f4 ♖d3+ 32 ♔b2 ♖h3 33 ♖e1 ♖h2+ 34 ♔b3 ♖h3+ 35 ♔c2 ♖h2+ 36 ♔d3 ♖h6 37 ♖fe4 c5 38 ♖xe6

The black pawns are insufficiently advanced to cause White any real problems.

38...♖h3+ 39 ♖1e3 ♖h1 40 ♖3e4 ♖h3+ 41 ♔c4 ♖g3 42 ♖h6 a6 43 ♖xh7 ♖g5 44 ♖b7 ♖h5 45 ♖e6 ♖h4+ 46 ♔d5 ♖b4 47 ♖c6 ♖d4+ 48 ♔e6 ♖b4 49 ♖b8 1-0

White will win easily by attacking the black pawns from the rear with his king.

To finish this section, here are two

games featuring slightly offbeat attempts by White.

1 d4 d5 2 c4 c6 3 ♘f3 ♘f6 4 ♘c3 dxc4 5 a4 ♗f5 6 ♘e5 e6 7 f3 ♗b4 8 ♗g5

Fighting for e4 by pinning the black knight, so that 9 e4 is now a threat. Instead 8 ♘xc4 0-0 9 ♗g5 h6 10 ♗h4 was met by 10...c5! 11 dxc5 ♕xd1+ 12 ♔xd1 (12 ♖xd1 ♗c2! 13 ♖c1 ♗xa4! 14 ♗xf6 gxf6 15 ♖a1 ♗b3 16 ♘b6 ♘c6 17 ♘xa8 ♖xa8 gave Black excellent compensation for the exchange in Beliavsky- Bareev, USSR 1986) 12...♖d8+ 13 ♔c1 ♘c6! 14 e4 ♗h7 15 ♗f2 ♘d7! in Akopian-Oll, New York Open 1994. 15...♘d7! intends ...♘xc5, highlighting the weakness on b3, and ...f7-f5 activating the light-squared bishop on h7. After 16 ♗d3 ♗xc5! 17 ♗xc5 ♘xc5 18 ♗c2 f5! 19 exf5 ♘d4! Black stood clearly better.

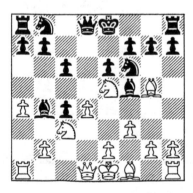

8...h6 9 ♗h4 c5 10 dxc5 ♕a5! 11 ♕d4 ♘c6 12 ♘xc6 bxc6 13 e4

♗xc5!

13...♗g6 14 ♗f2 is less good for Black.

14 ♕xc4 ♗g6 15 ♕a6 ♕xa6 16 ♗xa6 ♖b8!

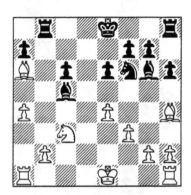

White already has trouble with his queenside.

17 ♘d1 ♘d7! 18 ♖c1 ♗b4+ 19 ♔f2 ♘c5 20 ♗e2 ♘xa4 21 ♖xc6 ♗c5+ 22 ♘e3 0-0 23 ♖a1 ♖b3 24 ♖xa4 ♗xe3+ 25 ♔g3 ♖xb2 26 ♗f1 f5!

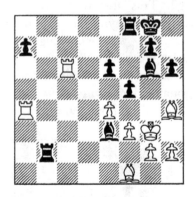

White is in big danger, but somehow he just hangs on.

27 ♖xe6 f4+ 28 ♔h3 ♗e8 29 ♖xe8 ♖xe8 30 ♗c4+ ♔h7 31 ♗d5 ♖e5 32 ♖c4 ♖h5 33 g3 ♖e5 34 ♖c7 ♖b6 35 ♖f7 ♔g6 36 ♖xa7 ♖b8 37 ♖d7 h5 38 ♗e7 ♖b2 39 ♗f8 fxg3 40 ♖xg7+

♔f6 41 ♖f7+ ♔g6 42 ♖g7+ ♔f6
½-½

1 d4 d5 2 c4 c6 3 ♘c3 ♘f6 4 ♘f3
dxc4 5 a4 ♗f5 6 ♘e5 e6 7 g3

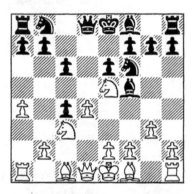

White fights for the e4-square in a different way: by putting the bishop on g2. This also helps to dissuade Black from playing the pawn break ...c6-c5, as b7 will be hanging.

7...♗b4 8 ♗g2 ♗e4!
Forcing White to block the long diagonal, which will allow Black to play ...c6-c5 without fear of ♗xb7.

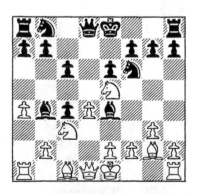

9 f3 ♗g6 10 0-0

10 e4 c5 11 ♗e3 cxd4 12 ♕xd4 ♕xd4 13 ♗xd4 ♘c6 14 ♘xc6 bxc6 15 0-0-0 0-0-0 is the theoretical recommendation, but 16 ♗f1 is more pleasant for White due to his superior structure and Black's inactive bishop on g6. 13...♘fd7!?, instead of 13...♘c6, was my first idea in order to reactivate the bishop on g6 with ...f7-f6 and ....♗f7. However, 14 ♘xc4 f6 15 0-0-0 ♘c6 16 ♗f2 (intending ...♘c6) 16...♔e7 17 ♘a2! wins the bishop pair, giving White a small advantage, as 17...♗c5 loses to 18 ♖xd7+! ♔xd7 19 ♗xc5, winning two pieces for a rook. In fact, 11...♕c7! is stronger: 12 ♘xc4 cxd4 (attacking the knight on c4) 13 ♕xd4 ♘c6 is fine for Black and 12 0-0 cxd4 13 ♗xd4 (13 ♘b5 ♕xe5 14 ♗f4 ♕c5 15 ♘c7+ ♔e7 16 ♘xa8 ♘a6! wins for Black) 13...♘c6 is also good.

10...c5 11 ♘a2 ♗a5

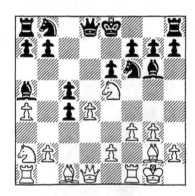

12 dxc5

Or 12 ♘xc4 cxd4 13 ♘xa5 ♕xa5 14 ♕xd4 ♘c6 15 ♕c4 ♕b6+ 16 ♔h1 ♘a5!, intending ...♘b3.

12...♕d5 13 ♕xd5 exd5 14 ♘xg6 hxg6 15 ♖b1 ♘bd7 16 ♗e3 ♖c8 17

b4 cxb3 18 ♘c1 b2 19 ♘b3 ♗c3 20 ♖fd1 ♘e5 21 ♗d4 ♗xd4+ 22 ♖xd4 b6 23 ♖xb2

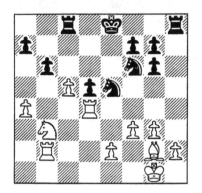

Better was **23 cxb6 axb6 24 ♖xb2**

♖c4 with an equal position according to Ivan Sokolov.

23...♘c4 24 ♖b1 bxc5 25 ♘xc5 0-0 26 ♘d3 ♘a3 27 ♖b7 ♘c2 28 ♖f4 ♖fe8 29 ♗h3 ♖c3

29...♖b8! (I.Sokolov) gave chances for an edge for Black.

30 ♔f2 g5 31 ♖f5 g4 32 ♗xg4 ♘e3 33 ♖xf6 ♘xg4+ 34 fxg4 gxf6 35 ♖xa7 ♖a3 36 ♘f4 ♖a2 37 a5 ♖e4 38 ♖a8+ ♔h7 39 ♖d8 ♖xa5 40 ♘xd5 ♖xd5 41 ♖xd5 ♖xg4 42 ♔f3 ♖a4 43 g4 ♔g6 44 h4 ♖a1 45 h5+ ♔g7 46 ♖f5 ♖g1 47 e3 ♖f1+ 48 ♔e4 ♖g1 49 ♖f4 ♖g3 ½-½

A tough endgame.

Summary

The sidelines do not seem to cause Black any problems, but undoubtedly the most crucial line at the moment is Kramnik's 14 ♔c2 ♘a6 15 ♘xc4 0-0-0 16 ♕e3. In general, such positions are easier to play for White than for Black.

1 d4 d5 2 c4 c6 3 ♘f3 ♘f6 4 ♘c3 dxc4 5 a4 ♗f5 6 ♘e5

6...e6 7 f3 *(D)*
> 7 g3 - *game 24*

7...♗b4 8 e4
> 8 ♗g5 - *game 23*

8...♗xe4 9 fxe4 ♘xe4 10 ♗d2 ♕xd4 11 ♘xe4 ♕xe4 12 ♕e2 ♗xd2+
13 ♔xd2 ♕d5+ 14 ♔c2
> 14 ♔c3 - *game 16*

14...♘a6 15 ♘xc4 0-0-0 16 ♕e5 *(D)*
> 16 ♕e3
>> 16...♔b8 - *game 17*
>> 16...♘c5 - *game 22*

16...f6 17 ♕e3
> 17 ♕xd5 - *game 18*

17...♔b8
> 17...c5 - *game 19*

18 ♗e2 *(D)*
> 18...♕xg2 - *game 20*
> 18...e5 - *game 21*

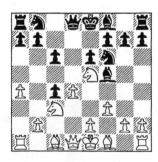

7 f3

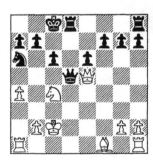

16 ♕e5

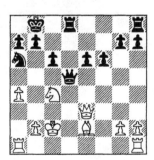

18 ♗e2

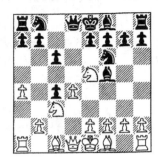

CHAPTER FOUR

The New Main Line: Black counterattacks

1 d4 d5 2 c4 c6 3 ♘f3 ♘f6 4 ♘c3 dxc4 5 a4 ♗f5 6 ♘e5

In this chapter we consider lines in which Black does not doggedly fight on for e4, but switches his attention to the d-pawn, arguing that 6 ♘e5 has weakened White's control of d4. Recent attention has concentrated on 6...e6 7 f3 c5!? 8 e4 cxd4, which is a specialty of both Boris Gelfand and Alexei Shirov. In the following games you will see the wildly different ways in which they handle this line!

> ### Game 25
> ### Piket-Gelfand
> *Wijk aan Zee 1996*

---

1 d4 d5 2 c4 c6 3 ♘f3 ♘f6 4 ♘c3 dxc4 5 a4 ♗f5 6 ♘e5 e6

In the 1920s and 1930s, 6...♘bd7 7 ♘xc4 ♕c7 8 g3 e5 (attacking d4) was popular, but after 9 dxe5 ♘xe5 10 ♗f4 ♖d8 11 ♕c1 ♗d6 12 ♘xd6+ ♕xd6 13 ♗g2, White stands better. He has the two bishops and Black cannot activate his queenside pawn majority.

7 f3 c5 8 e4 cxd4 9 ♗xc4!?

An unusual move that was successful in its first appearance in Khalif-

man-Salov, 1991, but had not been tried since, as, in his notes, Khalifman had pointed out a continuation that seemed to equalise for Black.

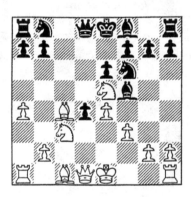

9...♗g6 10 ♗b5+ ♘fd7

10...♘bd7?? simply loses to 11 ♗g5.

11 ♕xd4 a6!

And this was it. If now 12 ♗e2, then 12...♘xe5 13 ♕xe5 ♘c6 is very good for Black, so White is forced into exchanges.

12 ♗xd7+ ♘xd7 13 ♕xd7+ ♕xd7 14 ♘xd7 ♔xd7 15 ♔e2 ♗b4 16 ♖d1+ ♔e7 17 ♗f4 ♖hc8 18 ♖ac1 ½-½

White obviously has more crucial possibilities. Who better to test the black position than Garry Kasparov?

> ## Game 26
> ### Kasparov-Shirov
> *Dos Hermanas 1996*

1 d4 d5 2 c4 c6 3 ♘f3 ♘f6 4 ♘c3 dxc4 5 a4 ♗f5 6 ♘e5 e6 7 f3 c5 8 e4 cxd4 9 exf5

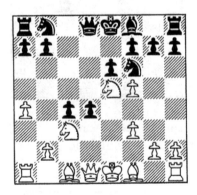

The main line and the only real test of Black's play.

9...♗b4!?

Black could not take the knight on c3, regaining his piece, because after 9...dxc3 10 ♕xd8+ ♔xd8 11 ♘xf7+ White wins a rook. However, if we imagine that it is Black's move after 9...♗b4, then 10...dxc3 is possible because after 11 ♕xd8+ ♔xd8 12 ♘xf7+

♔e7 13 ♘xh8, 13...cxb2 is discovered check, so Black wins. White can try 10 ♔f2!?, since after 10...dxc3 11 ♕xd8+ ♔xd8 12 ♘xf7+ ♔e7 13 ♘xh8, 13...cxb2 is no longer discovered check, but Black can exploit the other exposed piece in White's position: the knight on e5. He can play 10...♕c7!, threatening both 11...♕xe5 and 11...dxc3, as White can no longer exchange queens with ♕xd8+. It seems that White can stop both these threats with 11 ♕xd4, but Black has the last laugh after 11...♗c5, picking up the queen. Sadly Black is not completely winning after 10...♕c7, as White can play 11 ♘a2, attacking the bishop on b4, but after 11...♕xe5 12 ♘xb4 ♕c5! Black has powerful compensation for the piece: two pawns and the exposed white king. I think that Black is better here. Garry played the more natural...

10 ♗xc4 ♕d6!?

An amazing move, adding to the confusion by attacking another piece.

11 ♗b5+ ♘c6 12 ♘c4 ♕c5?

A serious and, in such a sharp position, fatal mistake. Black could simply have retreated with 12...♕d7 when, due to the threat of ...d4xc3, White probably has nothing better than to repeat moves with 13 ♘e5 ♛d6.

13 ♗d2!

Black cannot regain the piece now, as 13...dxc3 14 bxc3 ♗a5 loses a piece to 15 ♘xa5. Obviously Shirov did not miss this move; but I believe that he overlooked something extremely cunning later on.

13...0-0 14 ♘a2 ♗xd2+ 15 ♛xd2 ♘e7

Black's is threatening ...a7-a6, winning the bishop, while he can also try ...♘xf5, intending ...♘e3. White seems to have problems but...

16 ♛b4!

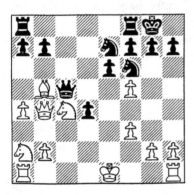

Forcing the exchange of queens as 16...♛xf5 allows 17 ♛xe7.

16...♛xb4+ 17 ♘xb4 a6 18 ♘b6!

White does not lose the bishop after all! The rest is easy for Kasparov.

18...axb5 19 ♘xa8 ♖xa8 20 fxe6 bxa4 21 exf7+ ♔xf7 22 ♔d2 ♔e6 23 ♖hc1 ♔d6 24 b3 b5 25 bxa4 bxa4 26 ♖c4 ♘f5 27 ♘c2 ♘d7 28 ♖cxa4 ♖xa4 29 ♖xa4 ♘b6 30 ♘xd4 1-0

A fine game by Kasparov, but not one that refutes Black's idea. Let us take another look.

Game 27
Gelfand-Shirov
Dortmund 1996

1 d4 d5 2 c4 c6 3 ♘c3 ♘f6 4 ♘f3 dxc4 5 a4 ♗f5 6 ♘e5 e6 7 f3 c5 8 e4 cxd4 9 exf5 ♗b4 10 ♗xc4 ♛d6

Shirov could not resist trying this idea a second time, but this time he is convincingly mauled. I do wonder why Black has been avoiding 10...dxc3 11 ♛xd8+ ♔xd8 12 0-0 (12 ♘xf7+ ♔e7 13 ♘xh8 cxb2+) 12...cxb2 13 ♗xb2 ♔e7 14 fxe6 fxe6.

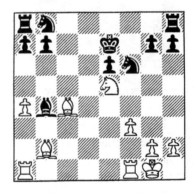

White's two bishops, the weak (but extra) pawn on e6 and the slightly exposed king on e7 obviously offer compensation for the pawn, but I don't see an advantage for White. Black's bishop on b4 prevents his opponent from playing ♖e1 and ganging up on e6, so 15 ♘d3 is tempting: 15...♗d6 is met by 16 ♖fe1 while 15...♗a5 16 ♗a3+ is also sub-optimal, as Jon Speelman would say! However, 15...♖c8!, attacking the bishop on c4, is the best defence: 16 ♘xb4 ♖xc4 is

good for Black and 16 &xe6 &xe6 17 ②xb4 leaves an equal position. Finally, 16 &b3 is met by 16...②c6, protecting the bishop, when 17 ②xb4 ②xb4 18 &fe1 &c6! (the point of 15...&c8) 19 &a3 a5!, intending ...&f7, is fine for Black. I feel that the onus is on White to demonstrate more than just sufficient play for the pawn.
11 &b5+ ②c6 12 &f4!

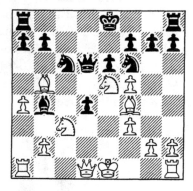

This prevents the capture 12...dxc3 due to 13 ②xc6 cxb2+ 14 ②xb4+!, when, thanks to the great strength of the discovered check, White wins the whole house!
12...0-0 13 ②xc6 &xf4 14 &xd4! &xc3+ 15 bxc3 &g5 16 f4 &xg2 17 0-0-0! bxc6 18 &hg1!

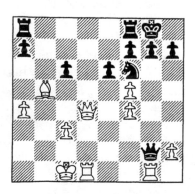

Suddenly it is Black's king that is in danger!
18...&xh2 19 &xc6 &ac8 20 &xf6 &xf4+ 21 &c2 g6 22 &df1 &h2+ 23 &g2 &h3 24 fxg6 fxg6

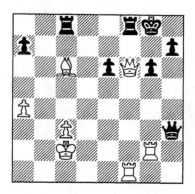

25 &xg6+ hxg6 26 &xg6+ &h8 27 &h1!
Winning the queen. The game is over.
27...&f2+ 28 &b3 &b8+ 29 &a3 1-0

So it seems as if, despite these two reverses, Shirov's 9...&b4 may well be just about playable. Let us now take a look at the more restrained continuation 9...②c6.

> ### Game 28
> ### Illescas-Gelfand
> *Dos Hermanas 1996*

1 d4 d5 2 c4 c6 3 ②f3 ②f6 4 ②c3 dxc4 5 a4 &f5 6 ②e5 e6 7 f3 c5 8 e4 cxd4 9 exf5 ②c6

see following diagram

The older and more solid move.
10 ②xc6 bxc6 11 fxe6 fxe6 12 &xc4

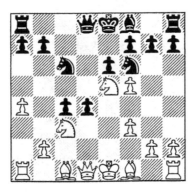

12 ♕e2 is considered in Game 30, while more adventurous players may like to consider the alternative 12 ♘a2 d3, keeping the piece and hoping to unravel later with g2-g3, ♗g2 and 0-0, although Black's counterplay is very dangerous!

12...dxc3 13 ♕xd8+ ♚xd8 14 bxc3

White is a bit better in this ending, since he has a slightly better pawn structure (fewer pawn islands) and the two bishops, but Black's pieces are active.

14...♘d5 15 ♚d2 ♗d6 16 ♚c2 ♚d7!

The king protects both weak pawns and helps to cover the only open file on the board: the b-file.

17 ♗d2 ♖hf8 18 ♖ab1 ♖ab8 19

♖xb8 ♖xb8 20 g3 ♗a3 21 ♖b1 ♖xb1 22 ♚xb1 ♗c5 23 ♗d3 h6 24 c4 ♗b4 25 cxd5 ½-½

> ## Game 29
> ### Van der Sterren-Petursson
> *San Bernardino Open 1992*

1 d4 d5 2 c4 c6 3 ♘c3 ♘f6 4 ♘f3 dxc4 5 a4 ♗f5 6 ♘e5 e6 7 f3 c5 8 e4 cxd4 9 exf5 ♘c6 10 ♘xc6 bxc6 11 fxe6 fxe6 12 ♗xc4 dxc3 13 bxc3

A different move-order that should be met by 13...♕xd1+ 14 ♚xd1 ♚d7, with the same ideas as in Illescas-Gelfand above.

13...♕a5? 14 ♕e2!!

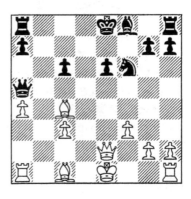

This rook sacrifice is a magnificent concept!

14...♕xc3+ 15 ♚f1 ♕xa1 16 ♕xe6+ ♚d8

16...♗e7 loses to 17 ♕xc6+ ♚f8 18 ♕xa8 ♘e8 19 ♚e2 ♕xa4 20 ♕d5 ♘d6 21 ♗d3 with a crushing attack (Petursson).

17 ♚e2!!

This quiet move, allowing the rook to join in the attack, justifies White's brilliant idea.

17...♕xa4 18 ♖d1+ ♕xd1+ 19 ♔xd1 ♗c5 20 ♕f7 ♖e8 21 ♕xg7 ♘d7 22 ♗f7 ♖f8 23 ♗e6 ♘f6 24 ♕b7 ♖e8 25 ♕xa8+ ♔c7 26 ♗f4+ 1-0

> *Game 30*
> ## Topalov-Gelfand
> *Dos Hermanas 1996*

1 d4 d5 2 c4 c6 3 ♘f3 ♘f6 4 ♘c3 dxc4 5 a4 ♗f5 6 ♘e5 e6 7 f3 c5 8 e4 cxd4 9 exf5 ♘c6 10 ♘xc6 bxc6 11 fxe6 fxe6 12 ♕e2!?

An interesting novelty that aims for a slightly different endgame.

12...dxc3 13 ♕xe6+ ♕e7 14 ♗xc4 ♕xe6+ 15 ♗xe6 cxb2 16 ♗xb2 ♗b4+ 17 ♔e2 ♔e7 18 ♗c4

This ending is somewhat more awkward for Black since his king is a little more open. Nonetheless, it is surprising how quickly his position goes downhill.

18...♖hd8?!

Black must try and activate his knight: 18...♘d5! is stronger, when 19 ♗xg7 ♖hg8! regains the g2-pawn. After 19 ♖ac1, 19...♖he8 is best, preventing 20 ♗xd5 cxd5 21 ♖c7+ due to 21...♔d6+, a discovered check that wins the rook!

19 ♖hd1 ♖ab8 20 g3

This places the g-pawn on a protected square and thus prevents the black knight from moving. Black now has serious problems which he is unable to overcome.

20...h5 21 ♖d4 ♗a5 22 ♗a3+ ♔e8 23 ♖ad1 ♖xd4 24 ♖xd4 ♖b1 25 ♗d3 ♖e1+ 26 ♔f2 ♔f7 27 ♗c5 ♖a1 28 ♗c4+ ♔e8 29 ♗d3 ♔f7 30 ♗xa7 ♖a2+ 31 ♔f1 ♖a1+ 32 ♔g2 ♖a2+ 33 ♔h3

Now White is just winning.

33...♖a3 34 f4 ♗e1 35 ♗c5 ♖c3 36 ♗c4+ ♔e8 37 ♗b4 ♖c1 38 ♗xe1 ♖xe1 39 a5 ♖a1 40 a6 ♔e7 41 ♖d2 1-0

Both 6...e6 7 f3 ♗b4 and 6...e6 7 f3 c5 are popular counterattacking systems at all levels of play. However, Black can also play more slowly, aiming to break out from a cramped position.

Game 31
Kramnik-Short
Novgorod 1994

---

1 ♘f3 d5 2 d4 ♘f6 3 c4 dxc4 4 ♘c3 c6 5 a4 ♗f5 6 ♘e5 ♘bd7 7 ♘xc4 ♘b6 8 ♘e5 a5

Preventing a4-a5-a6, breaking up the black queenside. 8...e6 is considered in the next game, while 8...♘bd7, still seeking the exchange of knights, was crushed by 9 ♕b3! ♘xe5 10 dxe5 ♘g4 11 ♕xb7 ♘xe5 12 f4 ♘g6 13 e4 ♗d7 14 f5 ♘e5 15 ♗f4 f6 16 ♗xe5 fxe5 17 ♖d1 in Kasparov-Timman, Riga 1995.

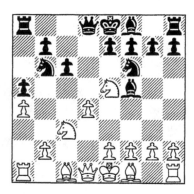

9 g3!?

A novelty. 9 f3 ♘fd7 10 ♘xd7 ♘xd7 11 e4 ♗g6 12 ♗e3 e6 13 ♗c4 ♗b4 14 0-0 is normal, with a slight advantage for White.

9...e6 10 ♗g2 ♗b4 11 0-0 0-0 12 e3 h6 13 ♕e2! ♗h7 14 ♖d1!

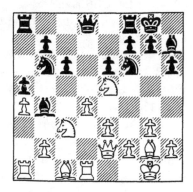

The standard plan of development: the queen supports e3-e4 from e2, leaving the rook to cover d4 from d1.

14....♘fd7 15 ♘d3!?

15 ♘xd7 ♘xd7 16 e4 is also slightly better for White.

15...♕e7 16 e4 e5 17 d5 ♖fd8 18 ♗e3?!

A mistake, allowing Black to weaken the white queenside. 18 ♗d2 would have kept an edge according to Kramnik.

18...♗xc3 19 bxc3 cxd5 20 exd5 ♘c4!?

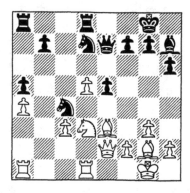

I think that Short may have missed White's next, but this is actually a good move!

21 ♗xh6 gxh6 22 ♕g4+ ♕g5 23

♕xc4 ♖ac8 24 ♕b5 ♖xc3

Black has good counterplay in this murky position.

25 ♘e1 b6 26 d6 e4 27 ♖d5 ♕f6 28 ♖ad1 e3 29 fxe3 ♖xe3 30 ♘d3 ♕c3 31 ♘f4 ♗e4 32 ♖5d2 ♕c5 33 ♕xc5 ♘xc5 34 ♗xe4 ♖xe4 35 ♘d5 ♔f8 36 ♘xb6 ♘xa4 37 ♘xa4 ♖xa4 38 ♖d5

White has a tiny edge in the endgame but he is unable to make anything of it.

38...♖d7 39 ♔g2 ♖a2+ 40 ♔h3 a4 41 ♖a5 a3 42 g4 ♔g7 43 ♔g3 ♔g6 44 h3 ♔g7 45 ♔h4 ♔g6 46 ♖a8 ♔h7 ½-½

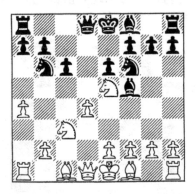

> ### Game 32
> ### Ruzele-Thorsteins
> *Lyon (European Club Cup) 1994*

1 d4 d5 2 c4 c6 3 ♘c3 ♘f6 4 ♘f3 dxc4 5 a4 ♗f5 6 ♘e5 ♘bd7 7 ♘xc4 ♘b6 8 ♘e5 e6!?

9 f3

A sensible reply. 9 a5 ♘bd5 (threatening ...♘b4 or ...♗b4) 10 a6!? is consistent but very risky, while 9 g3 is met by 9...♗b4 10 ♗g2 ♘e4 when the natural 11 ♗d2 loses to 11...♘xf2!

12 ♔xf2 ♕xd4+ and ...♕xe5.

9...a5 10 e4

10 g4 ♘fd5! 11 h4 (11 gxf5 ♕h4+ 12 ♔d2 ♕f4+ wins back the piece) 11...f6 12 gxf5 fxe5 (Ruzele) is extremely unclear.

10...♗g6 11 ♗e3 ♗b4 12 ♗e2 0-0?!

12...♘fd7 is better since 13 ♘xg6 hxg6 gives Black play on the h-file, while 13 ♘xd7 ♘xd7 transposes to 8...a5 9 f3.

13 0-0 ♘fd7

Now White can take the two bishops.

14 ♘xg6! hxg6 15 ♔h1 ♕e7 16 ♗g1 ♖fd8 17 ♕b3

White has effortlessly obtained a wonderful version of the old main line with 6 e3.

17...c5 18 ♘a2! cxd4 19 ♘xb4 ♕xb4 20 ♕xb4 axb4 21 a5 d3 22 ♗xd3 ♘e5 23 ♗b5 ♘bc4 24 f4 ♘d6 25 ♗e2 ♘c6 26 ♗b6 ♖e8 27 e5 ♘c8 28 ♗f3 ♘xb6 29 axb6 ♘e7 30 ♗xb7 ♖ab8 31 ♖a7 ♘c8 32 ♗xc8 ♖exc8 33 ♖c7 ♖xc7 34 bxc7 ♖c8 35 ♖c1 ♔f8 36 ♔g1 ♔e7 37 ♔f2 ♔d7 38 ♔e3 ♖xc7 39 ♖xc7+ ♔xc7 40 ♔d4 ♔b6 41 ♔c4 1-0

Model strategy by White.

Summary

6...e6 7 f3 c5 should definitely be studied by Black players. I particularly like Shirov's handling of the line with 8 e4 cxd4 9 exf5 ♗b4. 9...♘c6 is for the calmer players amongst you who don't mind taking on a slightly worse ending. Probably it is important to choose the right opponent: 9...♘c6 will be ideal against an impatient attacking player, while 9...♗b4 would unsettle a more positionally inclined player.

If you prefer the more solid 6...♘bd7 7 ♘xc4 ♘b6, and don't mind the slightly cramped positions that arise from this line, then Thorsteins's 8...e6 looks like a good move-order, since it avoids Kramnik's 9 g3.

1 d4 d5 2 c4 c6 3 ♘f3 ♘f6 4 ♘c3 dxc4 5 a4 ♗f5 6 ♘e5

6...e6
     6...♘bd7 7 ♘xc4 ♘b6 8 ♘e5 *(D)*
          8...a5 - *game 31*
          8...e6 - *game 32*
7 f3 c5 8 e4 cxd4 9 exf5 *(D)*
     9 ♗xc4 - *game 25*
9...♘c6
     9...♗b4 10 ♗xc4 ♕d6 11 ♗b5+ ♘c6
          12 ♘c4 - *game 26*
          12 ♗f4 - *game 27*
10 ♘xc6 bxc6 11 fxe6 fxe6 *(D)* 12 ♗xc4
     12 ♕e2 - *game 30*
12...dxc3
     13 ♕e2 - *game 28*
     13 bxc3 - *game 29*

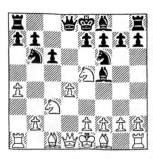

8 ♘e5

9 exf5

11...fxe6

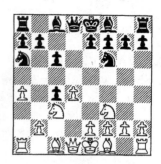

CHAPTER FIVE

The Smyslov Variation

1 d4 d5 2 c4 c6 3 ♘f3 ♘f6 4 ♘c3 dxc4 5 a4 ♘a6

The move 5...♘a6 was originally an idea of Emanuel Lasker; and it was later taken up and played with success by another World Champion Vassily Smyslov. Recently Ivanchuk and Short have also used it to good effect.

Question 1: 5...♘a6 looks a little strange. What does it do?

Answer: 5 a4 (preventing ...b7-b5) has weakened the b4-square. In the main lines with 5...♗f5 6 e3, Black puts a bishop on b4 and develops his queen's knight to d7; here, Black leaves his bishop on e7 to keep b4 free for the knight. Black's light-squared bishop will now go to g4 to put pressure on the d4-square.

Question 2: So what difference does this make?

Answer: In the 6 e3 lines, Black's bishops on f5 and b4 combine to prevent White from easily achieving e3-e4. In this line, Black exerts virtually no pressure on e4, and very little on d4, which means that White pretty much has the centre to himself.

Question 3: Well that doesn't sound very promising for Black, does it? What am I supposed to do as Black?

Answer: Smyslov's style as Black is perfectly reflected in this system: he is prepared to accept a slight space disadvantage and will just place his pieces on good squares where they coordinate well with each other. Since Black's position is very solid, the opponent will not be able to launch a sudden attack and Smyslov will patiently unravel, gaining space little by little until he frees himself.

> ### Game 33
> ### Ivanchuk-Smyslov
> *Tallinn (rapidplay) 1996*

1 d4 d5 2 ♘f3 ♘f6 3 c4 c6 4 ♘c3 dxc4 5 a4 ♘a6 6 e4

Very straightforward play.

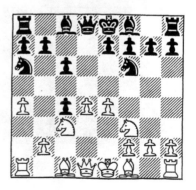

6...♗g4 7 ♗xc4 ♗xf3

7...e6 is dealt with in the next game.

8 gxf3 e6 9 ♗xa6 bxa6

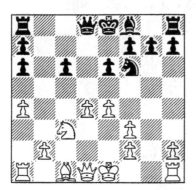

Black has no problems here. First, he has exchanged two sets of minor pieces, and such exchanges always help the player with less space, since it means that there are fewer pieces in a confined area; second, Black's doubled a-pawns give Black the b-file on which to activate his major pieces and attack the vulnerable white queenside. Black would be much less active if his a6-pawn were on b7! Certainly Ivanchuk is happy to exchange queens and escape with a draw.

10 ♕e2 a5 11 ♕c4 ♖c8 12 ♖g1 g6 13 ♔f1 ♗g7 14 ♕c5 ♕b6 15 ♕xb6 axb6 16 ♗e3 0-0 17 ♖c1 ♘d7 ½-½

If Black delays exchanging on f3, a more complex situation arises, as we shall see in the next game.

Game 34
Novikov-Gretarsson
Berlin Open 1995

---

1 d4 d5 2 c4 c6 3 ♘f3 ♘f6 4 ♘c3 dxc4 5 a4 ♘a6 6 e4 ♗g4 7 ♗xc4 e6

A different approach which leads to a complicated middlegame.

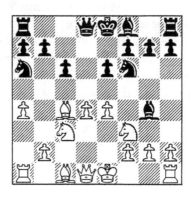

8 ♗e3 ♘b4 9 a5

A typical idea from White, aiming to prevent either ...♕a5, activating the black queen, or ...a7-a5, cementing the knight on b4. Black has to be a little careful that this knight, protected only by the bishop on e7, does not get cut off from the rest of his army.

9...♗e7

9...♗xf3, forcing 10 gxf3 (10 ♕xf3 ♘c2+), was still possible but Black prefers natural development.

10 ♗e2 0-0 11 0-0 b5!

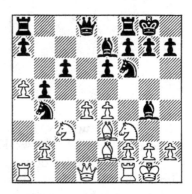

This far from obvious move is the black plan for survival in these middlegames.

Question 4: What is the point of this move?

Answer: The main idea is that Black gains just a little more space for his pieces – remember what I said about Smyslov patiently improving his position, taking extra territory little by little. The other point is that Black would like to strike at the white centre with ...c6-c5, but first he needs a reasonable square for his queen: he can't put it on the c- or d-files, since after ...c5xd4 these files will be opened and the queen will be in the firing line of white rooks on d1 and c1. 11...b5 frees b7 for the black queen, where it is absolutely safe. A nice bonus is that after ...c6-c5, the black queen will join with the knight on f6 in attacking the e4-pawn.

12 ♕b3 ♕c7 13 ♖fc1 ♕b7 14 ♗g5 ♖fd8 15 ♗xf6 gxf6

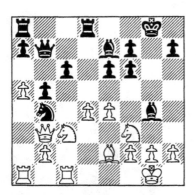

A forced recapture as 15...♗xf6 loses a piece to 16 ♕xb4. The weakening to Black's kingside is not too serious, however, since White has no pieces in that area. Moreover, without his dark-squared bishop, White loses a lot of control over the central dark squares, which means that d4 is

weaker and hence it is easier for Black to achieve the ...c6-c5 break.

16 ♘e1 ♗xe2 17 ♘xe2 ♖ac8 18 ♖c3 c5! 19 dxc5 ♘a6!!

A very neat idea. 19...♗xc5 would have lost to 20 ♖xc5 ♖xc5 21 ♕xb4.

20 ♘d3 ♘xc5 21 ♘xc5 ♖xc5 22 ♖xc5 ♗xc5 23 ♕c3 ♕xe4 24 ♕xf6 ♕d5 25 ♘c3 ♕d4 26 ♕f3 ♕e5

Black's control of the dark squares gives him good chances.

27 g3 b4 28 ♖d1 ♖xd1+ 29 ♘xd1 ♗d4 30 ♕d3 ♔g7 31 b3 h6 32 a6 ♗c5 33 ♔f1 ♔f6 ½-½

This game is a model illustration of Black's middlegame strategy in this variation.

Now we move on to look at 6 e3.

Game 35
Benz-Gretarsson
Oberwart Open 1996

1 d4 d5 2 ♘f3 ♘f6 3 c4 c6 4 ♘c3 dxc4 5 a4 ♘a6 6 e3

The most solid option and probably the best move. White does not give Black the chance to double his f-pawns with ...♗xf3.

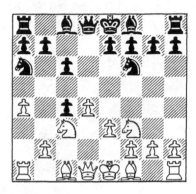

6...♗g4 7 ♗xc4 e6 8 h3 ♗h5 9 0-0 ♘b4 10 ♕e2!

A typical manoeuvre in queen's pawn openings: the queen moves to e2, supporting the e4 push, while the rook is played to d1, supporting the d4-pawn and discouraging ...c6-c5 due to the opposition of the rook to the black queen on d8.

10...♗e7 11 ♖d1 0-0 12 g4 ♗g6 13 e4 c5!?

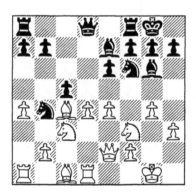

An unusually active move at this stage of the Smyslov variation, but Helgi Gretarsson, a fanatic of this variation, has an interesting idea in mind. The more restrained 13...♘d7 is considered in the next two games.

14 d5!?

A very sharp reply, but I would be intrigued to discover what Helgi had in mind against the *ECO* recommendation of 14 ♗f4! (taking c7 away from the queen) 14...♕a5 15 ♘d2!, intending ♘b3 to harass the queen some more. 15...cxd4 16 ♘b3 ♕b6 17 a5 is not nice for Black and the reckless 15...♘c2 loses a piece to 16 ♘b3 ♕b4 17 ♘a2 ♕xa4 18 ♘c3! (18 ♕xc2 ♗xe4 causes some problems) 18...♕b4 19 ♖a4 ♕b6 20 ♕xc2.

14...exd5! 15 e5 d4!? 16 exf6 ♗xf6 17 ♗f4

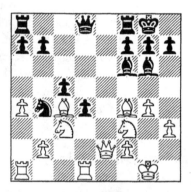

Question 5: What is going on?

Answer: As compensation for the piece, Black has two pawns, a strong centre and a tempo on the queen with ...♖e8. Unfortunately, I don't think that this is quite enough; and this is almost entirely due to the bad placing of the bishop on f6, which takes away a brilliant square for the black queen. Perhaps Black could try 15...♖e8!? to meet 16 exf6 (16 ♗b5 ♘c6) with either 16...♗d6 or 16...♗f8, intending to recapture on f6 with the queen, though I would be the first to admit that it all looks a bit speculative!

17...♖e8 18 ♕f1 a6

To prevent ♘b5.

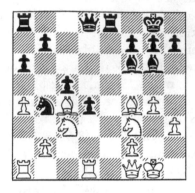

19 ♖d2?!

White starts to go wrong around here and drifts very quickly into a lost position. 19 ♘a2! ♘d5 (19...♘c6 20 ♖e1! beginning to exchange pieces) 20 ♗g3, intending ♖e1, would have given White the better chances.

19...♕d7 20 ♕g2? ♕c6 21 ♘b5 axb5 22 ♗xb5 ♕e4 23 ♗xe8 ♕xf4 24 ♖e1 h6 25 ♗b5 ♗e4 26 ♖xe4 ♕xe4 27 ♗c4 ♕f4 28 b3 ♖e8 29 ♕g3 ♕xg3+ 30 fxg3 ♘c6 31 ♗d5 ♘a5 32 b4 ♖d8 33 ♗e4 cxb4 34 ♘e1 b3 35 ♗d3 ♗g5 36 ♖b2 ♖c8 37 ♔f1 g6 38 ♔e2 ♗c1 39 ♖b1 b2 40 ♘f3 ♘b3 0-1

The main line for Black is considered in the next game, probably the finest blindfold game ever played. I wish I could play this well in normal chess!

> ### Game 36
> ### Kramnik-Ivanchuk
> *Monte Carlo (blindfold) 1996*

1 ♘f3 d5 2 d4 ♘f6 3 c4 c6 4 ♘c3 dxc4 5 a4 ♘a6 6 e3 ♗g4 7 ♗xc4 e6

8 h3 ♗h5 9 0-0 ♘b4 10 ♕e2 ♗e7 11 ♖d1 0-0 12 g4 ♗g6 13 e4 ♘d7!?

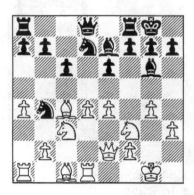

Black anticipates the threat of ♘e5 and f2-f4, intending f4-f5 to trap the bishop on g6.

14 ♘e5!?

A very double-edged decision. White allows his central pawns to be doubled, but also frees the f-pawn to advance.

14...♘xe5 15 dxe5 ♕a5 16 f4 ♖ad8 17 ♗e3 h6!

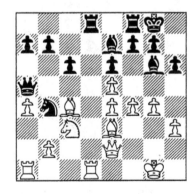

Making an escape square for the bishop.

18 ♔g2 ♗h7 19 ♖xd8 ♖xd8 20 ♖d1 g5!

20...a6 is considered in the next game.

21 ♖xd8+ ♗xd8 22 ♕d2 gxf4 23 ♗xf4 ♗b6 24 ♗b5!!

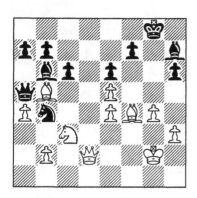

24 ♗xh6 allows 24...♕xe5, so White sacrifices a bishop to keep the queen boxed in on a5.

24...cxb5 25 ♗xh6 ♗c5 26 ♕d7 ♗g6 27 ♕c8+ ♔h7 28 ♗g5

With his threat of ♗f6 and ♕h8 mate, White just seems to be winning, but now it is Black's turn to sacrifice a piece, this time to free his queen.

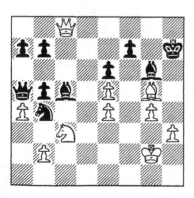

28...♘d5!! 29 ♕xc5

Not 29 exd5 when 29...♕b4! launches a powerful counterattack.

29...♘xc3 30 ♕xc3 ♕xa4 31 ♔g3 ♕xe4 32 ♗f6 b4 33 ♕c8 ♕e1+ 34 ♔f4 ♕f2+ 35 ♔g5 ♕d2+ 36 ♔h4 ♕h6+ 37 ♔g3 ♕e3+ ½-½

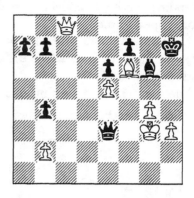

Black must give perpetual check due to the threat of mate on h8.

> ### Game 37
> ### Kramnik-Short
> *Moscow (Intel Grand Prix) 1996*

1 ♘f3 d5 2 d4 c6 3 c4 ♘f6 4 ♘c3 dxc4 5 a4 ♘a6 6 e3 ♗g4 7 ♗xc4 e6 8 h3 ♗h5 9 0-0 ♘b4 10 ♕e2 ♗e7 11 ♖d1 0-0 12 g4 ♗g6 13 e4 ♘d7 14 ♘e5

Kramnik obviously believes in this continuation for White, but it seems a little hasty to me. Since Black is threatening little in the centre, a sensible move like 14 ♗f4, taking c7 away from the black queen and intending perhaps h3-h4-h5, makes more appeal to me.

14...♘xe5 15 dxe5 ♕a5 16 f4 h6 17 ♔g2 ♖ad8 18 ♗e3 ♗h7 19 ♖xd8 ♖xd8 20 ♖d1 a6!

The new idea, activating Black's queenside majority.

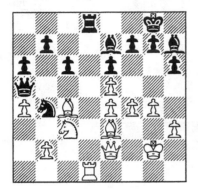

21 ♗b3 ♔h8!

So that the bishop on h7 can reactivate itself by means of ...♗g8, ...f7-f6 and ...♗f7! This position would not be to everyone's taste, but Short wins a nice game.

22 ♖d2 b5 23 axb5 cxb5 24 f5 ♘c6!

Stressing the new weakness on e5.

25 ♖xd8+ ♕xd8 26 ♗f4 ♗c5 27 ♗e3 ♕b6 28 ♗xc5 ♕xc5 29 ♕f2

♕xe5 30 ♕b6 ♘d4 31 ♗d1 ♗g8!

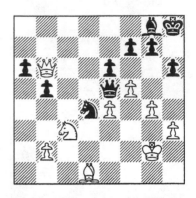

32 ♗f3 f6! 33 ♘e2 ♘xe2 34 ♗xe2 ♕xe4+ 35 ♗f3 ♕c2+ 36 ♕f2 ♕xf2+ 37 ♔xf2 a5 38 fxe6 ♗xe6!

Yes it's free! White will not be able to cope with the two potential outside passed pawns.

39 ♔e3 b4 40 ♗d1 f5 41 ♔f4 fxg4 42 hxg4 ♔g8 43 ♔e5 ♔f7 44 ♔d6 ♔f6 45 b3 g5 46 ♔c5 ♔e5 47 ♔b5 ♔d4 48 ♔xa5 ♔c3 49 ♔a4 ♗d5 0-1

Kramnik's approach with ♘e5 is rather impatient. A quieter method is demonstrated in the following game, the last of a match between France's 13-year-old star Etienne Bacrot and ex-World Champion Vassily Smyslov, whose name this variation bears. The match score was a rather crushing 5-1, and one player was made to look vastly inferior in the endgame. But not the player one might have expected!

1 d4 d5 2 c4 c6 3 ♘c3 ♘f6 4 ♘f3 dxc4 5 a4 ♘a6 6 e3 ♗g4 7 ♗xc4 e6 8 0-0 ♗e7 9 ♕e2 ♘b4 10 ♖d1 0-0 11 h3 ♗h5 12 a5!?

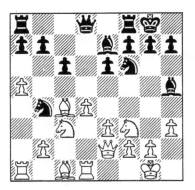

We have already seen White's idea in Novikov-Gretarsson. Our first thought should be therefore to implement the plan of ...b7-b5, followed by the transfer of the queen to b7: 12...b5 13 ♗b3 ♕c7 14 e4 (14 g4 ♗g6 15 ♘e5!?, intending a quick h3-h4-h5 trapping the bishop) 14...♕b7. It is obvious that White is better prepared for his opponent's plan than in the above game. The rook covers d4 from d1, while the queen on e2 both protects e4 and attacks b5, making ...c6-c5 more difficult to achieve. After 15 g4 ♗g6 16 ♘e5 White intends either f2-

f4-f5 or h3-h4-h5 with a clear advantage. Black must play ...♘d7 to prevent ♘e5, either before or after ...b7-b5, with a typical 5...♘a6 position.

12...♖c8?! 13 ♗b3 c5?

This is excessively active from Black at this early stage.

14 ♘b5!

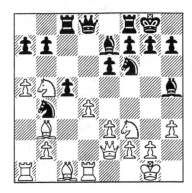

This fine move threatens ♘xa7 and d4xc5 followed by ♘d6.

14...♗xf3 15 gxf3 a6 16 dxc5 ♘bd5 17 ♘d6 ♗xd6 18 cxd6 ♕xd6 19 ♖a4 ♖c5 20 f4 ♕c6 21 ♗d2 ♕b5 22 ♕xb5 ♖xb5

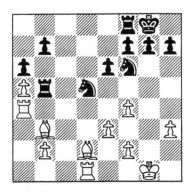

The ending is very nasty for Black, since his knights have no outposts.

23 ♖a3 ♘e4 24 ♗e1 ♘df6 25 ♖c1 ♖d8 26 f3 ♘d6 27 ♖d1 ♘fe8 28

♗a4 ♖d5 29 ♖xd5 exd5 30 ♖d3
♘c7 31 ♗b4 ♘db5 32 ♗c5 f5 33
♗b6 ♖d6 34 e4!

37 ♔f2 ♘xc7 38 ♖b3 ♘e6 39
♖xb7+ ♔f8 40 ♖b8+ ♔e7 41 ♖b7+
♖c7 42 ♖xc7+ ♘xc7 43 ♗c6 d4 44
b4 1-0

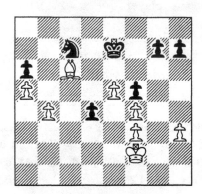

This allows White to make a massive stride forwards with his e-pawn as 34...dxe4 loses a piece to 35 ♖xd6.
34...♔f7 35 e5 ♖c6 36 ♗xc7 ♖c1+

A fine victory for the young Frenchman, crowning an amazing match result.

Summary

Theoretically, 5...♘a6 is doing well for Black and if a system has been played by Smyslov, Ivanchuk and Short then it must have some merit! If you don't mind playing slightly cramped positions, then it could be the system for you. 6 e3 is the most critical test.

1 d4 d5 2 c4 c6 3 ♘f3 ♘f6 4 ♘c3 dxc4 5 a4 ♘a6

6 e4 *(D)*

    6 e3 ♗g4 7 ♗xc4 e6 8 h3 ♗h5 9 0-0 ♘b4 10 ♕e2 ♗e7 11 ♖d1 0-0

        12 g4 ♗g6 13 e4 *(D)*

            13...c5 - *game 35*

            13...♘d7 14 ♘e5 ♘xe5 15 dxe5 ♕a5 16 f4 ♖ad8 17 ♗e3 h6

            18 ♔g2 ♗h7 19 ♖xd8 ♖xd8 20 ♖d1

                20...g5 - *game 36*

                20...a6 - *game 37*

        12 a5 - *game 38*

6...♗g4 7 ♗xc4 *(D)*

    7...♗xf3 - *game 33*

    7...e6 - *game 34*

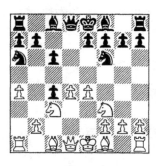

6 e4

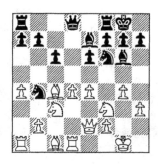

13 e4

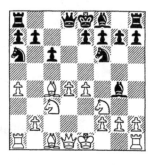

7 ♗xc4

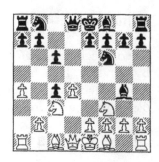

CHAPTER SIX

The Bronstein Variation

1 d4 d5 2 c4 c6 3 ♘f3 ♘f6 4 ♘c3 dxc4 5 a4 ♗g4

Like Smyslov's 5...♘a6, 5...♗g4 is a variation that has been around for a long time without ever gaining widespread popularity.

Question 1: What is the point of 5...♗g4?

Answer: 5...♗g4 looks to delay e3-e4 by putting pressure on the d4-pawn. White should avoid 6 e4 as after 6...e6 7 ♗xc4 ♗b4 (threatening ...♘xe4), he has problems holding his centre. Therefore 6 ♘e5, gaining a tempo on the bishop, is almost always played. Now after 6...♗h5 White still cannot play 7 e4, as this would allow 7...♗xd1!

Question 2: What plans does White have?

Answer: Since White can take the c4-pawn at his leisure, there is no need for him to hurry with ♘xc4. His two most dangerous plans both aim to exploit the slightly precarious position of the bishop on h5:

a) 7 f3, which blocks the h5-d1 diagonal and threatens to achieve e2-e4, while supporting g2-g4 ♗g6, h2-h4, intending to trap the bishop.

b) 7 h3, intending to gain space on

the kingside with g2-g4 and develop the bishop to g2. This variation is so complicated, however, that a whole book would be needed to explain its ramifications! I will do my best, but I'm afraid you'll only get a brief taster!

For the less savage, there is also the quiet 7 g3, planning a fianchetto.

> *Game 39*
> **Kramnik-Damljanovic**
> *Moscow Olympiad 1994*

1 d4 d5 2 ♘f3 ♘f6 3 c4 c6 4 ♘c3 dxc4 5 a4 ♗g4 6 ♘e5 ♗h5 7 f3 ♘fd7

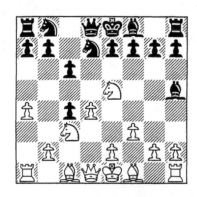

Question 3: This is a strange-looking move. What does it do?

Answer: Black must challenge the knight on e5 or his bishop will be caught by g2-g4 and h2-h4. Now after 8 g4, 8...♗g6 9 h4 ♘xe5! 10 dxe5 ♕xd1+ 11 ♔xd1 h5 is fine for Black. However, another point is to give Black an unexpected opportunity to continue his pressure against the d4-pawn.

8 ♘xc4 e5!

And this is it! The knight's move from f6 has freed the h4-d8 diagonal for the queen, giving Black the opportunity to exploit the slight weakening on the e1-h4 diagonal created by 7 f3.

9 ♘e4

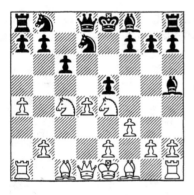

The old move and a very sensible one. White cannot play 9 dxe5 as 9...♕h4+! wins the knight on c4, while 9 ♘xe5 ♘xe5 10 dxe5 ♘d7 11 f4 ♗b4 is a very risky pawn grab. Black has a substantial lead in development and will follow up with ...♕e7 and ...f7-f6 or ...g7-g5, opening further lines. 9 g3 is considered in Games 41 and 42.

Question 4: What does 9 ♘e4 do?

Answer: Black's pieces are a little strange at the moment: his king's knight is on d7, which is the queen's knight's natural square, while his bishop is biting granite on h5. 9 ♘e4 seeks to exploit this temporary confusion by threatening a devastating check on d6, and also shields the knight on c4 along the fourth rank; so 10 dxe5 is now a threat as ...♕h4+ will no longer achieve anything.

9...♗b4+ 10 ♗d2 ♕e7 11 ♗xb4 ♕xb4+ 12 ♕d2 ♕xd2+

Forced, as 12...♕xc4 loses to 13 ♘d6+.

13 ♔xd2 exd4 14 ♘ed6+ ♔e7

The alternative, the enterprising 14...♔d8, is considered in the next game.

15 ♘f5+ ♔f6 16 ♘xd4 ♖d8

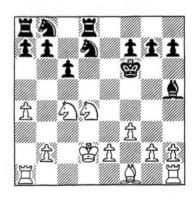

We have reached an ending, but the tactical complications continue for some while yet.

17 ♔c3 ♘c5 18 e4! ♖xd4 19 ♔xd4 ♘b3+ 20 ♔c3 ♘xa1 21 ♗e2 ♔e7 22 ♖xa1 ♘d7 23 b4!

Question 5: Isn't this just a boring, equal ending?

Answer: Unfortunately for Black, no. White does enjoy a definite edge here, and it all boils down to that wayward bishop on h5. First, Black is going to have to spend a tempo with

...f7-f6 to bring it back into play; and second, if it was still on c8, Black wouldn't have such an annoying weakness on b7! The white knight is excellently placed on c4, as it can attack b7 via d6 (with the help of a rook on d1) or a5.

Question 6: You mean Black is lost?!

Answer: No, not at all. He only has one real weakness, so he should be able to defend, but it isn't really that much fun.

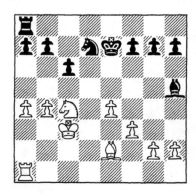

23...f6 24 ≝d1 ♘b6

Kramnik suggests that 24...≝b8 is more solid.

25 ♘a5!

Exchanging knights would greatly simplify Black's defensive task. Now White forces unpleasant weaknesses in the black queenside.

25...♘xa4+ 26 ♔b3 ♘b6 27 ♘xb7 ♗f7+ 28 ♔c3

The trade of the a4-pawn for the b7-pawn has been profitable for White, as now he has two targets: a7 and c6.

28...≝b8 29 ♗a6 ♗e8 30 ≝a1 ♘d7 31 f4!

Gaining space on the kingside and

stopping the knight from activating via e5. Black obviously felt very uncomfortable round here, since he starts just moving his knight around for no reason.

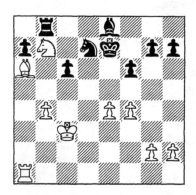

31...♘b6 32 ♘c5 ♘d7 33 ♘b3 g6 34 ♘d4 ♘b6 35 ♗c4 ≝b7 36 ♗b3 ♗d7 37 ≝a5!

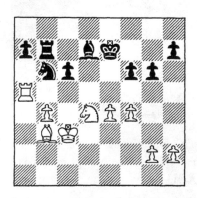

Threatening a breakthrough with e4-e5.

37...♘a8? 38 ♗a4 ≝c7 39 ≝c5 ♘b6 1-0

And Black lost on time in this hopeless position: he is just going to lose his c-pawn.

Let us now take a look at 14...♔d8 instead of 14...♔e7.

Game 40
Schandorff-Hellsten
Copenhagen 1996

1 d4 d5 2 c4 c6 3 ♘f3 ♘f6 4 ♘c3 dxc4 5 a4 ♗g4 6 ♘e5 ♗h5 7 f3 ♘fd7 8 ♘xc4 e5 9 ♘e4 ♗b4+ 10 ♗d2 ♕e7 11 ♗xb4 ♕xb4+ 12 ♕d2 ♕xd2+ 13 ♔xd2 exd4 14 ♘ed6+ ♔d8!?

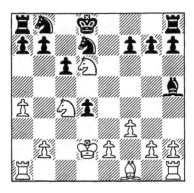

An interesting idea: in the ending above, Black would have loved to have his king on c7 protecting the weak b-pawn! One drawback is that White can take on b7 with check, but at least the position is unbalanced, unlike the safe edge which White easily obtained in the game Kramnik-Damljanovic.

15 ♘xb7+

15 g4!? ♗g6 16 f4 f6 17 f5 ♗e8 18 ♘xb7+ ♔c7 19 ♘ba5 does not really improve the white position, but instead 15 h4!? (threatening g2-g4 and h4-h5) 15...f6 16 g4 ♗e8 17 ♘f5!?, attacking g7 and d4, is an interesting attempt.

15...♔c7 16 ♘ba5 ♘a6 17 e4 dxe3+ 18 ♘xe3 ♘b4

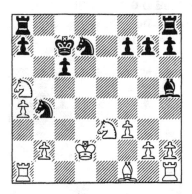

19 ♔c3 ♖he8! 20 ♘ac4 ♖ab8 21 ♗d3? ♘xd3 22 ♔xd3 ♘c5+ 23 ♔e2 f5! 24 ♔f1 f4 25 ♘d1 ♘b3 0-1

An amazingly quick defeat for White!

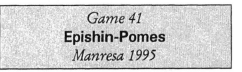

Game 41
Epishin-Pomes
Manresa 1995

1 d4 d5 2 c4 c6 3 ♘f3 ♘f6 4 ♘c3 dxc4 5 a4 ♗g4 6 ♘e5 ♗h5 7 f3 ♘fd7 8 ♘xc4 e5 9 g3

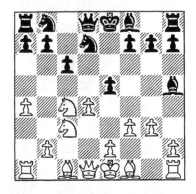

This has been the most popular choice recently. White prevents ...♕h4+ and threatens d4xe5.

9...♗b4

For 9...f6 see Game 43.

10 dxe5 0-0 11 ♗h3!?

White now threatens e5-e6.

11...♕e7 12 f4

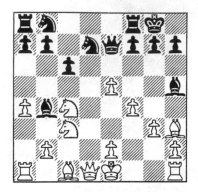

12 ♗f4 is considered in the next game.

12...♖d8 13 ♕c2 f6

Absolutely necessary in order for Black to free himself.

14 e6

14 exf6 ♘xf6 gives Black some counterplay for the pawn.

14...♘c5 15 ♘e3

Or 15 f5 ♖d4 16 ♘e3 ♘ba6 17 0-0 ♖ad8 with counterplay (Epishin).

15...♘xe6 16 ♘f5

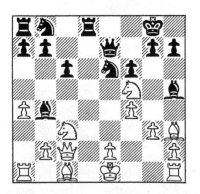

16...♕d7?!

A mistake according to Epishin. The alternative 16...♕e8 17 ♕e4 ♘a6

18 ♘h6+ gxh6 19 ♗xe6 ♗f7 20 f5 h5 21 0-0 would have led to a murky position.

17 ♗e3

17 ♕e4!, intending ♘h6+, was better.

17...♘a6 18 0-0 ♗f7 19 ♘e4 ♔h8 20 ♖ad1 ♕c7 21 b3 ♗f8 22 ♕b2 ♘ec5 23 ♘xf6 ♗xb3 24 ♖xd8 ♖xd8 25 ♘g4 ♗d5 26 ♘d4 ♘xa4?! 27 ♕a1 b5?

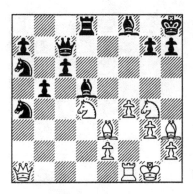

Black is determined to ignore his kingside defences. The punishment is swift.

28 f5 ♗b4 29 ♘e6! ♗xe6 30 fxe6 ♗c3 31 ♕b1 ♕e7 32 ♘h6!

The pawn capture 32...gxh6 loses to 33 ♖f7.

32...♖f8 33 ♘f7+ ♔g8 34 ♗f5 ♖xf7 35 ♗xh7+ ♔h8 36 ♖xf7 ♕e8 37 ♕f5 1-0

Game 42
Parker-Hellsten
Copenhagen 1996

1 d4 d5 2 c4 c6 3 ♘f3 ♘f6 4 ♘c3 dxc4 5 a4 ♗g4 6 ♘e5 ♗h5 7 f3 ♘fd7 8 ♘xc4 e5 9 g3 ♗b4 10 dxe5 0-0 11 ♗h3 ♕e7 12 ♗f4

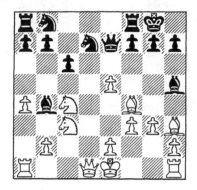

A very interesting idea. 12...g5, to chase the bishop away, is simply met by 13 ♗d2 (13 ♗xd7 ♘xd7 14 ♗xg5 ♕xg5 15 ♕xd7 b5 16 f4 is very messy) 13...♘xe5 14 ♘xe5 ♕xe5 15 ♘e4 ♗xd2+ 16 ♕xd2 g4 17 ♗g2 with a better position for White.

12...♖d8 13 ♕c2 ♗g6 14 ♗f5

14 e4 is very risky but not easy to refute. For example, 14...♕c5 15 ♘d6 ♘xe5 16 ♘xb7 (forking queen and rook) 16...♘xf3+ 17 ♔f1 ♕c4+ 18 ♕e2 seems fine for White, while 14...b5 15 axb5 cxb5 16 ♘e3 ♘xe5 17 0-0 is also difficult to judge.

14...♘b6 15 ♗xg6 hxg6 16 ♘xb6 axb6 17 h4

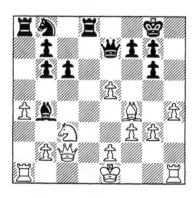

Preventing ...g7-g5.

17...♖e8

17...♘d7 fails to 18 ♗g5! ♕xe5 (18...f6 19 exf6 gxf6 20 ♕xg6+) 19 ♗xd8 ♕xg3+ 20 ♔f1 ♖xd8 21 ♘e4, when Black has insufficient compensation for the exchange.

18 0-0 ♕c5+ 19 ♔g2 ♗xc3 20 ♕xc3 ♕xc3 21 bxc3 ♘d7

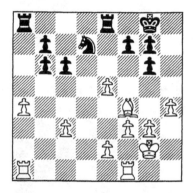

Black just manages to hold the ensuing endgame, but the whole line seems extremely uncomfortable for him.

22 ♖fb1 ♖a6 23 a5 ♖ea8 24 ♖d1 ♘f8 25 ♖ab1 b5 26 c4 bxc4 27 ♖xb7 ♖xa5 28 ♖b4 ♖d5 29 ♖c1 ♘d7 30 ♖bxc4 ♘xe5 31 ♗xe5 ♖xe5 32 e4 ♖a2+ 33 ♔h3 f5 34 ♖xc6 fxe4 35 fxe4 ♖xe4 36 ♖xg6 ♔h7 37 ♖g5 ♖e7 38 ♖h5+ ½-½

> ### Game 43
> **Dautov-Nikolic**
> *Ter Apel 1994*

1 d4 d5 2 c4 c6 3 ♘f3 ♘f6 4 ♘c3 dxc4 5 a4 ♗g4 6 ♘e5 ♗h5 7 f3 ♘fd7 8 ♘xc4 e5 9 g3 f6

A very solid continuation, just protecting the e5-pawn.

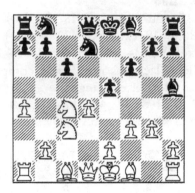

10 dxe5 ♞xe5 11 ♕xd8+ ♚xd8 12 ♞xe5 fxe5 13 ♗g5+ ♚c7 14 0-0-0 ♞d7 15 ♗h3 ♗e8 16 ♗e3!

This very nice move prepares f3-f4, breaking the position open.

16...♞c5 17 f4 ♗d7 18 ♗xd7 ♞xd7 19 f5

19 ♞e4 ♖e8 20 f5 was even more accurate. The ending is basically very pleasant for White.

19...♗e7 20 g4 h6 21 ♞e4 ♞f6 22 ♞xf6 ♗xf6 23 h4 ♗e7 24 ♗f2 ♖ad8 25 ♗g3 ♗f6 26 ♚c2 ♖xd1 27 ♖xd1 ♖g8 28 g5 hxg5 29 hxg5 ♗xg5 30 ♗xe5+ ♚c8 31 ♖g1 ♖e8 32 ♗xg7 ♖xe2+ 33 ♚d3 ♖d2+ 34 ♚c3 ♗e3 35 ♖g3 ♗f4 36 ♖f3 ♖g2 37 ♖xf4 ♖xg7 38 f6 ♖g8 39 ♚d4 ♚d7 40

♚e5 ♖e8+ 41 ♚f5 ♖e2 42 b4 ♚e8 43 ♖h4 ♖f2+ 44 ♚e6 ♖e2+ 45 ♚d6 a5 46 bxa5 ♚f7 47 ♖h7+ ♚xf6 48 ♖xb7 ♖e4 49 ♚xc6 ♖xa4 50 ♖b5 1-0

This is all very sensible. However, White has another rather crazy idea.

Game 44
Shirov-Nikolic
Wijk aan Zee 1993

1 d4 d5 2 c4 c6 3 ♞f3 ♞f6 4 ♞c3 dxc4 5 a4 ♗g4 6 ♞e5 ♗h5 7 f3 ♞fd7 8 ♞xc4 e5 9 e4

And this is it! This very natural move was completely ignored until recently.

9...♕h4+ 10 g3

The wacky 10 ♚e2 is considered in the next game.

10...♕f6!

Having softened up the kingside with ...♕h4+, the queen retreats to f6, where it helps attack f3 with the bishop on h5, and d4 with the pawn on e5.

11 dxe5! ♕xf3 12 ♞d6+! ♚d8

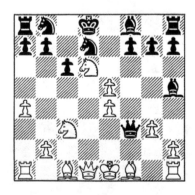

Amazingly, 12...♗xd6 loses to 13

♕xd6 ♕xh1 14 ♗g5 (threatening ♕e7+ mate) 14...f6 15 exf6 gxf6 16 ♕e6+ ♔d8 (16...♔f8 17 ♗h6+ mate) 17 ♗xf6+ ♘xf6 18 ♕xf6+ ♔c7 19 ♕e5+! followed by ♕xh5 or ♕xh8 with a crushing position, as pointed out by Ivan Sokolov.

13 ♕xf3 ♗xf3 14 ♘xf7+ ♔e8 15 e6!?

The first new move of the game! In I.Sokolov-Lautier, Belgrade 1991, White had played 15 ♘xh8 but 15...♘xe5! (Shirov) 16 ♗f4 ♘8d7 is nice for Black, as after 17 ♖g1, 17...♗c5! makes sure the rook does not escape.

15...♘c5 16 ♗c4 ♗xh1 17 ♘xh8 ♗xe4! 18 ♗g5

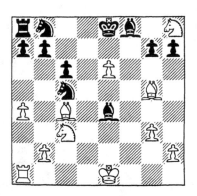

18 b4 seems to win a piece, but 18...♗d3! (Shirov) 19 e7 ♗xc4 (19...♗xe7 20 ♗f7+ followed by bxc5 keeps the fun going) 20 exf8♕+ ♔xf8 21 bxc5 ♔g8 favours Black.

18...♗f5 19 0-0-0 ♗e7 20 ♗xe7 ♔xe7 21 ♖f1 g6

A slight error according to Shirov. 21...♗e6 22 ♗xe6 ♔xe6 23 ♖f8 a5 is suggested instead, but this also seems quite nice for White.

22 g4 ♗xe6 23 ♗xe6 ♔xe6 24 ♖f8

a5 25 h4 b6 26 ♔c2?!

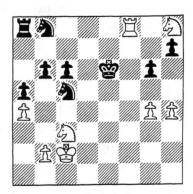

Either 26 ♔d2 or 26 g5 would have kept a slight advantage for White according to Shirov.

26...♘ca6 27 ♘e4 ♖a7 28 ♘g5+ ♔d5 29 ♘hf7 ♖e7 30 ♖h8 ♘d7 31 ♖xh7 ♘e5 32 ♘xe5 ♖xh7 33 ♘xh7 ♔xe5 34 ♘f8 ♔f4 35 ♘xg6+ ♔xg4 36 ♘e5+ ♔xh4 37 ♘xc6 ♔g5 ½-½

Game 45
Nesterov-Imanaliev
Bishkek Zonal 1993

---

1 d4 d5 2 c4 c6 3 ♘f3 ♘f6 4 ♘c3 dxc4 5 a4 ♗g4 6 ♘e5 ♗h5 7 f3 ♘fd7 8 ♘xc4 e5 9 e4 ♕h4+ 10 ♔e2!?

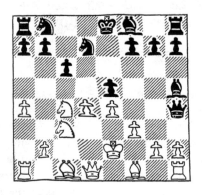

A magnificent idea, the tactical just-ification of which lies in my all-time favourite opening trap!

10...exd4

Tempting but not the best. Black should react more calmly with 10...♗b4, intending ...0-0.

11 ♕xd4 ♗c5 12 ♘d6+! ♔f8

12...♔e7 loses to 13 ♘f5+ while 12...♔d8 is met by 13 ♘xb7+.

13 ♕xg7+!!

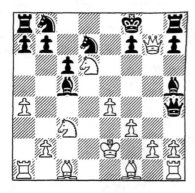

13...♔xg7 14 ♘f5+

Regaining the sacrificed queen and winning a pawn, with a good position to boot!

14...♔f6 15 ♘xh4 ♘a6 16 ♗h6 ♘e5 17 g4 ♘xg4 18 fxg4 ♗xg4+ 19 ♔d2 ♖ad8+ 20 ♔c2 ♘b4+ 21 ♔b3 ♗e6+ 22 ♗c4 ♗xc4+ 23 ♔xc4 ♖d4+ 24 ♔xc5 ♘c2 25 ♗g7+ 1-0

Finally, White can try the develop-ing move 9 ♗e3.

Question 8: This looks very strange, doesn't it?

Answer: With 9 ♗e3, White de-fends the d4-pawn and prepares to meet 9...♕h4+ with the simple 10 ♗f2. However, 10 dxe5 is still not a threat due to 10...♕h4+, winning the

knight on c4. The move is extremely aggressive: White will expand on the kingside with g2-g4 and h2-h4 and try to win Black's light-squared bishop, while rapid queenside castling is also on the agenda.

Game 46
I.Sokolov-Hellsten
Malmo 1995

1 d4 d5 2 c4 c6 3 ♘c3 ♘f6 4 ♘f3 dxc4 5 a4 ♗g4 6 ♘e5 ♗h5 7 f3 ♘fd7 8 ♘xc4 e5 9 ♗e3 ♗g6

Question 9: This looks odd as well!

Answer: This is a typical idea in this line. Black realises that the bishop is doing nothing on h5, where it merely bites against the pawn on f3. There-fore, he moves it to a more active di-agonal, delaying the decision of which piece to put on b4: the bishop on f8 or the knight on b8, via a6.

10 h4!

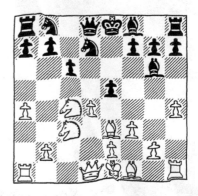

This not only aims to harass the bishop on g6 with h5, but also threat-ens d4xe5 by removing Black's re-source of ...♕h4+.

10...♗e7 11 h5! ♗f5

11...♗h4+ is met simply by 12 ♗f2

♗xf2+ 13 ♔xf2 ♗f5 14 ♘d6+, winning a piece.

12 dxe5 0-0 13 h6! ♘a6 14 hxg7 ♖e8 15 g4 ♗g6 16 f4!

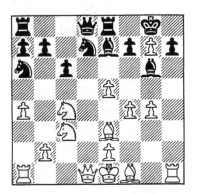

Quite amazing! White is only moving pawns, but Black just seems to be helpless!

16...♘b4 17 ♖c1 ♘d5 18 ♗g2 ♘xe3 19 ♘xe3 ♗h4+ 20 ♔f1 ♗g3 21 f5 ♕b6 22 fxg6 hxg6 23 ♕d2 ♗xe5 24 ♘ed5 1-0

24...cxd5 loses to either 25 ♖h8+ ♔xg7 26 ♕h6+ ♔f6 27 ♘xd5+, forking king and queen, or instead 25 ♘xd5 ♕d4 26 ♖h8+ ♔xg7 27 ♕h6+ mate! A game of astonishing ferocity, even by Ivan Sokolov's remarkable standards!

> ### Game 47
> ### Krasenkov-Sapis
> *Polish Championship 1995*

1 ♘f3 d5 2 d4 c6 3 c4 ♘f6 4 ♘c3 dxc4 5 a4 ♗g4 6 ♘e5 ♗h5 7 f3! ♘fd7 8 ♘xc4 e5 9 ♗e3 ♗b4

A more natural developing move than 9...♗g6.

10 g4 ♗g6 11 dxe5!

This is possible now, since 11...♕h4+ no longer hits the knight on c4!

11...0-0!?

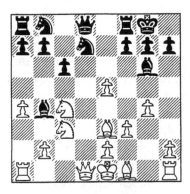

This is a new idea. The alternative 11...♕e7+ was played in the original game Granda Zuniga-Nikolic, Biel Interzonal 1993, and now 12 ♘d6+ ♗xd6 13 ♕xd6 would have given White a safe edge due to his two bishops and the weakness of Black's dark squares. Instead in the game, White went for the crazy complications of 12 f4 ♕h4+ 13 ♗f2 ♕xg4 14 ♕b3 ♘a6 15 ♘d6+ ♗xd6 16 ♕xb7 ♘b4 17 ♕xa8+ ♗b8 which is just unfathomable.

12 h4 h6 13 h5 ♗h7 14 g5!? hxg5 15 h6 g6

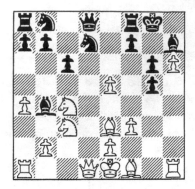

Question 10: Why is White playing so aggressively? He was a pawn up with more space; why did he sacrifice his g-pawn?

Answer: White has played some very strange moves in the opening. First, he put his bishop on e3 in front of the e-pawn, blocking in his light-squared bishop. Then, instead of developing his pieces, he advanced his kingside pawns in order to chase Black's light-squared bishop. White has won a pawn, but his pawn advances have left many weak squares in his position. For example, if Black could get a rook to d8 and then play ...♘c5, aiming for the weak b3-square, then White's position would become critical. White has raised the stakes with his risky opening play – he must continue in the same aggressive manner or Black will develop and exploit White's weaknesses.

16 ♖g1 ♕e7 17 ♖xg5 ♖d8 18 ♕c2 b5?

A tactical miscalculation. Chekhov recommends 18...♕e6! 19 ♕e4 ♘a6! (intending ...♘dc5) 20 ♕h4 b5!, when I think that Black has good counter-chances.

19 axb5 cxb5 20 ♕e4! bxc4 21 ♕xa8 ♘xe5 22 ♕xa7

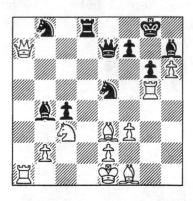

White is winning now due to his large material advantage.

22...♘bd7 23 ♕d4 f6 24 ♖g3 ♘c5 25 ♖a8! ♖xa8 26 ♕d5+ ♘e6 27 ♕xa8+ ♘f8 28 ♔f2 ♗d6 29 ♘e4 ♗b4 30 ♗d4 ♔h8 31 f4 ♘ed7 32 ♖e3 ♕f7 33 ♘g5 ♕g8 34 ♖e8 1-0

And now things get even more complicated. Let us take a look at 7 h3.

Game 48
Gelfand-Nikolic
Manila Interzonal 1990

---

1 d4 d5 2 ♘f3 ♘f6 3 c4 c6 4 ♘c3 dxc4 5 a4 ♗g4 6 ♘e5 ♗h5 7 h3 ♘a6 8 g4 ♗g6 9 ♗g2

I find it hard to recommend this line to players of either colour, unless they have six months in which to analyse the mind-boggling complications! 9 e3 is discussed in the next game.

9...♘b4 10 0-0 ♗c2 11 ♕d2 ♗b3

Question 7: Why is Black doing this?

Answer: If Black were to play normally, then White's space advantage would guarantee him a substantial advantage. Black therefore keeps the pawn and challenges White to make something of his lead in development.

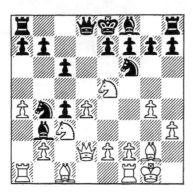

12 a5

Threatening a5-a6 to break up the black queenside. 12 ♘e4, attacking the knight on b4, is the other major continuation, aiming for the attractive trap 12...♘xe4 13 ♕xb4 ♘d6 14 ♕xb7!!, when 14...♘xb7 loses to 15 ♗xc6+.

12...a6

Stopping a5-a6, but in fact this may not be so dangerous: 12...e6 13 a6 ♕c7 14 axb7 ♕xb7 15 g5 ♘fd5 16 e4 ♘b6 17 d5 looks impressive, but 17...♖d8 18 ♘xc6 ♘xc6 19 dxc6 ♕xc6 20 e5 ♘d5 21 ♖xa7 ♗c5, with ...0-0 to follow, was nice for Black in the game Moreno-Rogers, Manila Olympiad 1992.

13 ♘a4 e6 14 g5 ♘d7 15 ♘xd7 ♕xd7 16 ♘b6 ♕d8 17 ♘xa8

see following diagram

17...♕xa8?

Ftacnik suggests 17...♘c2 18 ♖b1 ♕xa8 19 e3 ♗b4 20 ♕e2 ♕d8 21 ♗d2

♕xg5, which looks like good compensation to me.

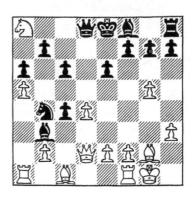

18 ♗e4 ♕d8 19 f4 ♗e7 20 e3 0-0 21 ♕e2 c5 22 dxc5 ♗xc5 23 ♗d2

Black does not really have enough for the exchange.

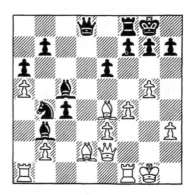

23...♘d5 24 ♔h1 ♕d7 25 ♖ac1 ♕a4 26 ♕f3 c3 27 bxc3 ♕xa5 28 f5 ♗c4 29 fxe6! ♘e7 30 ♗xh7+ ♔xh7 31 ♕e4+ ♘g6 32 ♕xc4 fxe6 33 ♕g4 ♖xf1+ 34 ♖xf1 ♕b5 35 c4 ♕c6+ 36 ♔g1 ♔g8 37 ♕f3 ♕d7 38 ♖f2 a5 39 ♕e4 ♘e7 40 ♗xa5 ♘f5 41 ♗d2 1-0

If White wishes to duck the critical lines that we saw in the previous game, he can play 9 e3 instead of 9 ♗g2.

Game 49
Klarenbeek-Rogers
Dutch Team Championship 1996

1 d4 c6 2 c4 d5 3 ♘f3 ♘f6 4 ♘c3 dxc4 5 a4 ♗g4 6 ♘e5 ♗h5 7 h3 ♘a6 8 g4 ♗g6 9 e3

A quieter attempt, making sure that White regains the pawn.

see following diagram

9...♘b4 10 ♗xc4 e6

10...♘c2+ loses to 11 ♕xc2 ♗xc2 12 ♗xf7 mate, but 10...♘d7 11 ♘xg6 hxg6 12 ♕f3, intending ♔f1-g2, is more normal. White has a small advantage here due to his slight space advantage and bishop pair.

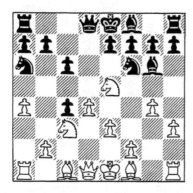

11 0-0 a5 12 f4 ♘d7 13 ♘xd7

Rogers recommends instead 13 e4 ♕h4 14 ♔g2 with a slight advantage for White, but with the threat of 15 ♘f3, intending f4-f5, this looks horrible for Black.

13...♗c2!

We have seen this before. Black makes sure that the bishop does not get shut in behind the e4-pawn. 13...♕xd7 is strongly met by 14 e4!

♘c2!? 15 ♕xc2 ♕xd4+ 16 ♔g2 ♕xc4 and 17 f5 (Rogers).

14 ♕e2 ♕xd7 15 ♘a2 ♗e4 16 ♘xb4?! ♗xb4 17 ♗d2 0-0 18 ♗xb4?!

White is just playing for a draw, but he is doing this badly. The text makes the a-pawn very weak.

18...axb4 19 b3 ♖a5! 20 ♖ad1 b5 21 axb5 cxb5 22 ♗d3 ♗b7!

Black is not going to exchange this bishop, while the a8-h1 diagonal is so tempting!

23 ♔h2 ♕d5 24 ♖b1 ♖c8 25 ♖fd1 g5!

An unexpected and really strong move.

26 ♖f1

26 fxg5 loses to 26...♕d6 (Rogers), as 27 ♔g1 ♕g3+ is terminal.

26...♖c3 27 ♖b2 gxf4 28 ♖xf4 ♖a1 29 ♔g3 ♖g1+ 30 ♔h4 h6 0-1

And White lost on time in this hopeless position.

Game 50
Leitao-Beliavsky
Erevan Olympiad 1996

1 d4 d5 2 c4 c6 3 ♘f3 ♘f6 4 ♘c3

dxc4 5 a4 ♗g4 6 ♘e5 ♗h5 7 g3

The quiet option. White ignores the bishop on h5 and just develops normally.

7...e6 8 ♗g2 ♗b4 9 ♘xc4 ♘d5

Attacking c3.

10 ♕b3 0-0 11 ♗d2

11 0-0 fails to 11...♗xc3 12 bxc3 ♗xe2, winning a pawn.

11...a5 12 e4 ♘b6!

An important and typical manoeuvre. Black exchanges a pair of knights, relieving his slightly cramped position while attacking d4.

13 ♘xb6

This rather helps Black. Beliavsky suggests 13 ♗e3 instead.

13...♕xb6 14 ♗e3 c5! 15 d5 ♘d7 16 0-0 ♘e5 17 h3 ♘f3+ 18 ♔h1 ♘d4

Clearly Black has now taken over the initiative. The bishop on h5 has suddenly become a major player, supporting the incursion of the black knight into the vulnerable kingside light squares.

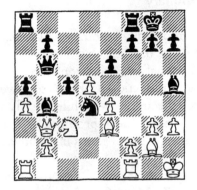

19 ♕c4 ♘c2 20 ♖ac1 ♘xe3 21 fxe3 ♕d6 22 ♔h2 ♖ae8 23 ♖ce1 ♗g6 24 ♖e2 ♖e7 25 ♘b5 ♕e5 26 ♗f3 ♖d7 27 ♔g2 ♔h8 28 ♘c3 ♖fd8 29 ♖d1 f6 30 ♖ed2 ♗f7 31 ♖d3 h5 32 ♕b5 c4 33 ♕xc4 h4 34 ♘e2 ♔h7 35 ♖d4 ♖c7 36 ♕d3 ♖dc8 37 gxh4 ♖c2 38 d6 ♖xb2 39 d7 ♖d8 40 ♔h1 ♗h5 41 ♗xh5 ♕xh5 42 e5+ f5 43 ♘g1 ♗c5 44 ♖g4 ♖xd7 45 ♕xd7 fxg4 46 ♕d3+ ♔h6 47 ♕c3 g3 48 ♕xb2 ♕xd1 49 ♔g2 ♕xa4 50 ♕xb7 ♕c2+ 51 ♔xg3 ♗xe3 0-1

A fine game by Beliavsky.

Summary

I cannot really recommend the 5...♗g4 line for Black, not because it is a particularly bad line, but simply because unless you have loads of time for detailed analysis, you won't be able to feel comfortable playing it. There are many theoretical problems to solve: 7 f3 ♘fd7 8 ♘xc4 e5 9 ♘e4 gives White a safe endgame edge, while 9 g3 is also dangerous. Even the crazy 9 e4 and 9 ♗e3 pose difficult problems! By contrast 7 h3 gives Black too many counterchances, while 7 g3 is a little tame.

1 d4 d5 2 c4 c6 3 ♘f3 ♘f6 4 ♘c3 dxc4 5 a4 ♗g4 6 ♘e5 ♗h5 7 f3

    7 h3 ♘a6 8 g4 ♗g6 *(D)*
        9 ♗g2 - *game 48*
        9 e3 - *game 49*
    7 g3 - *game 50*
7...♘fd7 8 ♘xc4 e5 *(D)* **9 ♘e4**
    9 g3
        9...♗b4 10 dxe5 0-0 11 ♗h3 ♕c7
            12 f4 - *game 41*
            12 ♗f4 - *game 42*
        9...f6 - *game 43*
    9 e4 ♕h4+
        10 g3 - *game 44*
        10 ♔e2 - *game 45*
    9 ♗e3
        9...♗g6 - *game 46*
        9...♗b4 - *game 47*

9...♗b4+ 10 ♗d2 ♕e7 11 ♗xb4 ♕xb4+ 12 ♕d2 ♕xd2 13 ♔xd2 exd4 14 ♘ed6+ *(D)*
    14...♔e7 - *game 39*
    14...♔d8 - *game 40*

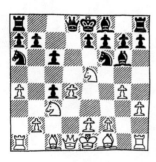

8...♗g6

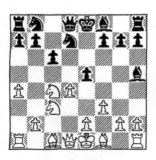

8...e5

14 ♘ed6+

CHAPTER SEVEN

The 4...a6 Slav: White plays 5 e3

1 d4 d5 2 c4 c6 3 ♘f3 ♘f6 4 ♘c3 a6

In the next two chapters we shall look at the move-order 1 d4 d5 2 c4 c6 3 ♘f3 ♘f6 4 ♘c3 a6.

Question 1: What is the point of 4...a6?

Answer: 4...a6 allows the bishop to develop outside the pawn chain to g4 or f5, since after ...♗f5, ♕b3 attacking b7 can be met by ...b7-b5, advancing the b7-pawn to a safe square, or ...♖a7!, an ugly looking but brilliant thought of Julian Hodgson's.

Question 2: Sounds great. Any drawbacks?

Answer: You had to ask. Black is placing a lot of pawns on light squares, so he can often suffer from weak dark squares.

Game 51
Oll-Anand
Biel Interzonal 1993

---

1 d4 d5 2 c4 c6 3 ♘f3 ♘f6 4 ♘c3 a6 5 e3

White protects the c4-pawn and prepares to develop his kingside. White's numerous alternatives here are discussed in the next chapter.

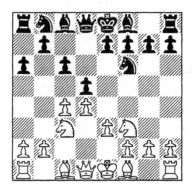

5...b5

Black would like to develop his bishop outside the pawn chain by playing 5...♗g4, for example, but 6 ♕b3 is strong, as 6...b5 7 cxd5 cxd5 8 a4! breaks up the black queenside. Black must be able to meet a2-a4 with ...b5-b4; after ...b5xa4, his a-pawn becomes very weak. In fact Black could play an interesting tactical idea here: after 8...♗xf3 9 gxf3 he can try 9...b4!?, so that after 10 ♕xb4, 10...e5! attacks the white queen. 11 ♕b3 exd4 12 exd4 ♘c6 13 ♗e3 ♗b4 gives compensation for the pawn due to White's weakened pawn structure, but 11 ♕b7! gains a tempo by attacking the rook on a8: 11...♘bd7 12 dxe5 ♘xe5 13 ♗xa6, when Black has enormous problems on the light squares. I'm sure that Julian Hodgson would suggest 6...♖a7(!), but after 7 ♘e5 (threatening 8 ♘xg4 ♘xg4 9 cxd5, winning a pawn) 7...e6 (as usual in the Slav Black does not mind swapping off his light-squared bishop for White's knight) 8 f3! ♗h5 9 g4 ♗g6 10 h4!, White's threat of h4-h5, trapping the bishop, forces Black to play the disastrous 10...h6, when 11 ♘xg6 fxg6 12 ♕c2 is just winning for White.

The inclusion of 5...b5 6 b3 takes the b3-square away from the white queen, allowing Black to develop his light-squared bishop in greater comfort.

6 b3

The exchange 6 cxd5 is considered in Game 55.

6...♗g4 7 h3

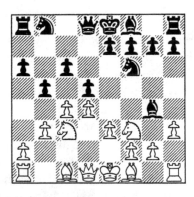

A very natural reaction, putting the question to the bishop. 7 ♗e2 is dealt with in Games 53 and 54.

7...♗xf3!

7...♗h5 8 g4 ♗g6 9 ♘e5, intending h2-h4, is rather awkward, as we have seen.

8 ♕xf3

For 8 gxf3, see the next game.

8...e6

This was a novelty at the time of the game, as black players had been experimenting with the violent 8...e5, to exploit the absence of the queen from the queenside and the slight weakness of the knight on c3 (it is no longer protected by a pawn on b2). I prefer Anand's simple move, which carries the same threats but without the risk.

9 ♗d2 ♗b4 10 ♕d1

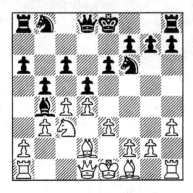

So that 10...♕a5 can be met by 11 ♕c2, but this move is a little meek. A few years ago, I played 10 ♗d3 ♕a5 11 ♖c1!? ♗xc3 12 ♖xc3 ♕xa2 13 ♕d1 against Jon Levitt, sacrificing a pawn in order to gain the advantage of two bishops against two knights. In fact I won a nice game after 13...0-0 14 0-0 ♕a3 15 ♕a1! ♕xa1 16 ♖xa1 ♖a7!? 17 cxb5 cxb5 (hoping for 18 ♗xb5 ♘e4, swapping off one of my bishops) 18 ♖c2!, allowing my dark-squared bishop to activate itself via b4. With control of the c-file and Black's passive pieces, I quickly gained a decisive advantage. Black should have played ...♘e4 at some point before ♖c2 in order to force the exchange of one of White's bishops, but White has reasonable compensation for the pawn.

10...0-0 11 ♗e2 bxc4! 12 bxc4 c5!

This is a typical freeing manoeuvre for Black. The immediate 11...c5 would of course have lost a pawn to 12 cxb5, so Black first exchanges on c4 and then breaks in the centre.

13 dxc5?

This is a serious mistake, and after Anand's superb play it almost looks like the losing move. White had to play for equality with 13 cxd5 cxd4 14 exd4 ♗xc3 15 ♗xc3 ♘xd5.

13...d4! 14 exd4 ♕xd4

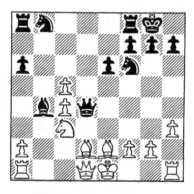

White has a worse pawn structure and real tactical problems, as Black's pieces quickly become amazingly active.

15 ♕c2

15 ♕c1 (to avoid Black gaining a tempo on the queen after ...♘c6-d4) 15...♖d8! prevents White from castling.

15...♘c6

15...♖d8 is well met by 16 ♖d1!

16 0-0 ♕e5!

Freeing the d4-square for the knight.

17 ♕a4 ♖ad8 18 ♗e1 ♘d4! 19 ♕xb4?

Retreating with 19 ♗d1 was the only (but rather miserable) way to avoid material loss.

19...♘xe2+ 20 ♘xe2

Or 20 ♔h1 ♖d3!

20...♕xa1 21 ♘c3 ♕c1 22 ♕a5 ♕f4 23 ♕xa6 ♖a8 24 ♕d6 ♕xc4 0-1

White had had enough. This game is a really impressive demolition job by Anand.

Let us now see what happens if Black recaptures on f3 with the pawn instead of the queen.

Game 52
Van der Sterren-Shirov
Biel Interzonal 1993

1 d4 d5 2 c4 c6 3 ♘f3 ♘f6 4 ♘c3 a6 5 e3 b5 6 b3 ♗g4 7 h3 ♗xf3 8 gxf3!?

The recapture with the queen leaves White vulnerable to a quick ...♗b4. This recapture aims to suffocate Black by playing f3-f4 (preventing Black's ...e7-e5 break) and c4-c5 (preventing the ...c6-c5 break).

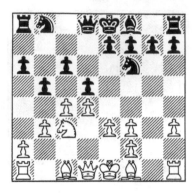

8...♘bd7!

Threatening ...e7-e5.

9 f4 bxc4 10 bxc4 dxc4!

By taking the c-pawn, Black prevents c4-c5. Now White cannot stop Black from playing ...c6-c5 himself, and the game soon fizzles out.

11 ♗xc4 e6

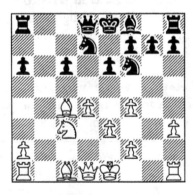

12 ♗d2 ♗b4 13 0-0 0-0 14 ♘e4 a5 15 ♗xb4 axb4 16 ♘xf6+ ♘xf6 17 ♕d3 ♘d5 18 ♖fc1 ♖a5 19 ♖ab1 ♕d6 ½-½

> ## Game 53
> ## Wells-Flear
> *Oakham 1994*

1 d4 d5 2 c4 c6 3 ♘c3 ♘f6 4 e3 a6

5 ♘f3 b5 6 b3 ♗g4 7 ♗e2

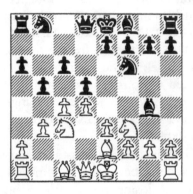

Peter Wells and Glenn Flear are well known for their deep knowledge of Slav systems, so this game is especially interesting.

7...e6 8 0-0 ♗d6?!

An inaccuracy that has unpleasant consequences. When White plays ♘e5, attacking c6, Black needs to be able to exchange it as quickly as possible for one of his own knights. Therefore Black should either play 8...♘bd7 or 8...♗e7 (to meet 9 ♘e5 with 9...♗xe2 10 ♕xe2 and then 10...♘fd7!). In the game, White gets a grip on the dark squares and wins in model fashion.

9 h3 ♗h5 10 ♘e5 ♗xe2 11 ♘xe2! 0-0 12 ♘f4 ♕c7 13 ♘fd3! ♘bd7 14 ♗b2 ♕b7 15 ♖c1 ♖ac8 16 ♖c2 ♖fd8 17 ♕f3 ♗f8 18 ♖fc1!

White's pieces are coordinating beautifully.

see following diagram

18...bxc4 19 bxc4 ♘xe5 20 ♘xe5 ♗d6 21 ♘d3 ♘e4 22 ♕e2 ♕b8 23 ♘c5 ♗xc5 24 dxc5 ♕b7 25 cxd5 ♖xd5 26 ♗xg7 ♔xg7 27 ♕g4+ ♘g5 28 e4 ♖e5 29 f4 ♖xe4 30 ♕xg5+

♔f8 31 ♖d2 ♕e7 32 ♕h6+ ♔g8 33 ♖c3 ♔h8 34 ♖g3 ♖g8 35 ♖d7 ♕xc5+ 36 ♔h2 1-0

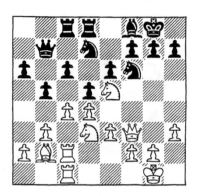

Game 54
Krasenkov-Epishin
Brno 1994

1 d4 ♘f6 2 c4 c6 3 ♘f3 d5 4 ♘c3 a6 5 e3 b5 6 b3 ♗g4 7 ♗e2 e6 8 h3 ♗h5 9 0-0 ♘bd7! 10 ♘e5 ♗xe2 11 ♘xe2 ♘xe5 12 dxe5 ♘d7

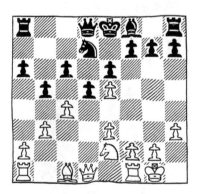

13 cxd5 cxd5 14 ♗b2 ♗e7 15 ♘d4 ♕b6 16 ♖c1 0-0 17 ♖c6

17 ♘c6 ♗c5 is equal according to Epishin. Here White's control of the c-file looks impressive, but with some fine moves, Epishin gradually pushes

White back.

17 ... ♕b7 18 ♕c2 ♖a7!!

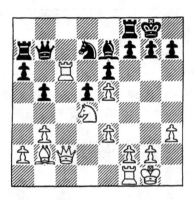

If White now defends the e5-pawn with 19 f4, then 19...♘b8! 20 ♖c3 b4! 21 ♖d3 ♖c8 (Epishin) gains the c-file for Black.

19 ♖c1 ♘xe5! 20 ♘xe6 ♕xc6 21 ♘xf8 ♕xc2 22 ♖xc2 ♘c4!! 23 bxc4 dxc4

The white knight is trapped. Black regains his piece and his queenside pawns prove to be far too much for his opponent to cope with.

24 ♗d4 ♖c7 25 ♘xh7 ♔xh7 26 ♗b6 ♖c6 27 ♗a5 ♗a3! 28 ♔f1 b4 29 ♔e2 ♖c5 30 ♗b6 ♖b5 31 ♗d4 b3 32 ♖xc4 b2 33 ♗xb2 ♖xb2+ 34 ♔f3 ♗b4 0-1

Instead of 6 b3, sometimes White plays 6 cxd5.

Game 55
Karpov-Short
Dortmund 1995

---

1 d4 d5 2 c4 c6 3 ♘c3 ♘f6 4 e3 a6
5 ♘f3 b5 6 cxd5 cxd5 7 ♘e5

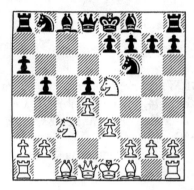

A different plan: White prevents the black bishop from developing outside the pawn chain and tries to prove that Black's queenside is weak.
7...e6 8 ♗d2 ♗e7 9 ♗e2 0-0 10 0-0 ♗b7 11 ♘d3
A typical manoeuvre by White, bringing the knight in contact with the weak c5-square.
11...♘bd7 12 b4 ♘b6!
White has weak squares too!
13 a4 ♘e4!

---

see following diagram

---

14 axb5 ♘xc3 15 ♗xc3 axb5 16 ♘c5 ♗c6 17 ♖xa8 ♕xa8 18 ♗d3 ♕a2 19 ♕h5 g6 20 ♕e5 ♕a7 21 ♖a1 ♕b8 22 ♕xb8 ♖xb8 23 ♖a5 ♗d8 24 ♗e1 ♖a8 25 ♖xa8 ♘xa8 26 g4 ♘b6 27 f3 ♘c4 28 ♗f2 ♗g5 29 f4 ♗e7 30 ♔g2 f6 31 ♔f3 ♔f7 32

♔e2 e5 33 h3 e4 ½-½

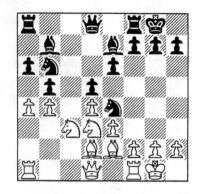

In the next game we see a tricky alternative move-order from White.

Game 56
Sadler-Hodgson
Hastings 1995/96

---

1 d4 d5 2 c4 c6 3 ♘c3
Of course playing 3 ♘c3 first gives Black the extra possibility of playing 3...dxc4 (see Chapter 10).
3...♘f6 4 e3 a6 5 ♕c2!?

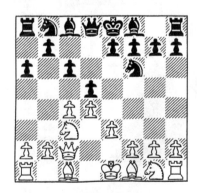

5 ♘f3 would of course simply transpose to the games we have already seen in this chapter. On c2 the white queen prevents Black from developing his bishop to f5, which

suggests that it would be natural for Black to put his bishop on g4 instead. However, after 5...b5 6 b3 ♗g4, White's idea is to play 7 ♘ge2, and if 7...♘bd7 then 8 h3 ♗h5 9 ♘f4, picking up the bishop pair.

Question 3: I thought you said that Black wanted to exchange off his light-squared bishop for White's knight! Aren't you contradicting yourself?

Answer: It is a conflict of ideas - as Black you say, 'The bishop on c8 was my problem piece and I'm glad I've exchanged it,' whereas with White you say 'Yes, I've won the bishop pair!' Frankly I would be happy to play either colour! It is clear, however, that in comparison with the line 5 ♘f3 b5 6 b3 ♗g4 7 h3 ♗xf3, White has gained the two bishops at a much lower cost: he has not had to either weaken his kingside pawn structure, or misplace his queen on the kingside. So basically White has got a good version of this typical sort of position. And that is the point of waiting with 5 ♕c2.

A similar idea for White is 5 ♗d3, preventing ...♗f5. Personally, I would grab this opportunity to transpose into a Queen's Gambit Accepted with 5...dxc4 6 ♗xc4 e6 7 ♘f3 c5, but I know that not everyone feels the same way! 5...♗g4!? 6 ♕b3 ♖a7 is possible, however, as neither 7 f3 dxc4 (7...♗h5 8 cxd5 cxd5 9 g4 ♗g6 10 ♗xg6 hxg6 11 g5 ♘h5 12 ♘ge2 [12 ♘xd5 ♘g3!] 12...e6 13 f4 is better for White due to the offside knight on h5) 8 ♗xc4 ♗h5, intending ...♘bd7 and ...e7-e5, nor 7 cxd5 cxd5 8 f3

♗c8!?, with ...♘c6 and ...e7-e5 to follow, is advantageous for White.

Right, back to the game!
5...e6 6 ♘f3 c5!

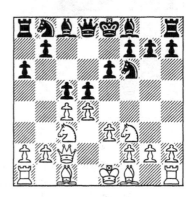

A very imaginative idea. Black totally changes his plan; he no longer plays for ...b7-b5, but strikes in the centre with ...c6-c5.

Question 4: Hasn't Black just wasted a move, since he's played first ...c7-c6 and now ...c6-c5?

Answer: This is true of course. White is playing the variation 1 d4 ♘f6 2 c4 e6 3 ♘f3 c5 4 e3 d5 5 ♘c3 a6, with the move ♕c2 added in for free. Black's contention is that this variation is not advantageous for White normally, and that the move ♕c2 does not make any difference in White's favour.

I felt that the best way to try to make use of ♕c2 was to play 7 cxd5, so that after 7...exd5 I could attack a clear target on d5 by bringing my rook to d1, exploiting the fact that my queen has already vacated this square. Moreover, my queen could be very useful on c2 to attack a bishop on c5 after d4xc5 ♗xc5.
7 cxd5 exd5 8 ♗e2 ♘c6 9 0-0 ♗e6!

The start of a superb tactical plan. Normal development could have easily ended in disaster. For example, if 9...♗e7 10 ♖d1 0-0 then 11 dxc5 ♗xc5 12 ♘xd5 wins a pawn, since the bishop on c5 hangs. Therefore Black begins a complicated tactical manoeuvre that seeks to exploit the exposed position of the queen on c2.

10 ♖d1 ♘b4! 11 ♕d2

11 ♕b1 ♕c8, threatening ...♗f5, could be embarrassing.

11...♘e4! 12 ♘xe4 dxe4

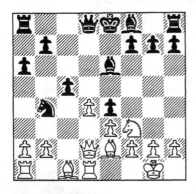

White's pieces are not coordinating well, and if White were to continue routinely with 13 ♘e5, then 13...cxd4 14 exd4 ♖c8, threatening ...♘c2, would be extremely annoying. Instead

of this defensive course, White plays for the initiative.

13 a3! exf3 14 ♗xf3 ♘c6!

Julian did not like the look of 14...♘d5 15 dxc5 ♘c7 16 ♗xb7 with three pawns and an initiative for the piece.

15 d5 ♘e5 16 dxe6 ♘xf3+ 17 gxf3 fxe6 18 b3 ♕xd2 19 ♗xd2

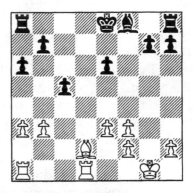

Black's queenside pawn majority even gives him a slight pull, but after a few adventures the game was eventually drawn.

19...♔d7! 20 ♗c3+ ♔c6 21 ♖a2 ♗e7 22 ♖ad2 ♖ad8 23 ♖xd8 ♖xd8 24 ♖xd8 ♗xd8 25 ♗xg7 c4!

Sacrificing a pawn to activate the king.

26 bxc4 ♔c5 27 f4 ♔xc4 28 e4 ♗c7 29 f5 exf5 30 exf5 ♔d5 31 a4 b5 32 axb5 axb5 33 ♗c3 ♗e5 34 ♗d2 ♔e4 35 ♔f1 ♔xf5 36 h3 ♗f4 37 ♗c3 ♔e4 38 ♔e2 ♗d6 39 ♗d2 ♔d4 40 ♗e3+ ♔c4 41 ♗d2 ♗b4 42 ♗xb4!

I spent a while just checking that the pawn ending was drawn. Remember that 41...b4 just leads to a draw after 42 ♗xb4 as Black has the wrong-coloured bishop for the rook's pawn!

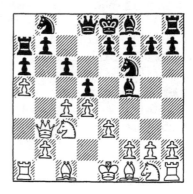

42...♔xb4 43 ♔d3 ♔a3 44 ♔c2 b4 45 ♔b1 ♔b3 46 h4 ♔c3 47 h5 ½-½

Since 47...h6 48 f4 ♔d4 49 ♔b2 ♔e4 50 ♔b3 ♔xf4 51 ♔xb4 ♔g4 52 ♔c3 ♔xh5 53 ♔d2 ♔g4 54 ♔e1 ♔f3 55 ♔f1 draws (just) for White.

Another tricky move for White is 5 a4.

Game 57
Atalik-Miles
Hastings 1995/96

1 d4 d5 2 c4 c6 3 ♘c3 ♘f6 4 e3 a6 5 a4

An unusual move in this position when White has already committed himself to e2-e3, shutting in his dark-squared bishop.

5...♗f5 6 ♕b3 ♖a7 7 a5!

Suddenly, to his horror, Miles realised that after the natural 7...e6, 8 ♕b6! is extremely strong, as after the forced 8...♕xb6 9 axb6 ♖a8 10 c5, intending b2-b4 and b4-b5 breaking through, White has a magnificent ending. Tony, practical as ever, just played a few necessary defensive moves and got on with the game!

7...♕d7 8 ♘f3 e6 9 ♘e5 ♕c8 10 f3 ♘fd7 11 ♘xd7 ♘xd7

Also possible was 11...♕xd7!?

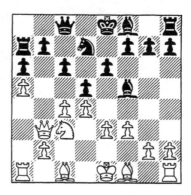

12 cxd5 cxd5 13 e4 dxe4 14 fxe4 ♗g6 15 e5! ♗e7 16 ♗e2 0-0 17 0-0 ♖a8 18 ♗e3 ♖b8 19 ♕a4 ♕d8 20 ♖ad1 ♖c8 21 d5 ♗c5 22 ♗f2 ♗xf2+ 23 ♖xf2 ♘c5 24 ♕b4 ♕g5 25 dxe6 fxe6 26 ♖xf8+ ♔xf8 27 ♕d4 ♔g8 28 ♗c4 ♕e7 29 b4 ♘d7 30 ♗b3 ♘f8 31 ♕d6 ♕e8 32 ♗a4 ♕f7 33 ♖f1 ♗f5 34 ♘e4 ♕g6 35 ♘c5 h6 36 ♗d1 ♗e4 37 ♖f2 ♗d5 38 ♗c2 ♕g5 39 h3 ♕e3 40 ♕e7 ♔h8 41 ♕f7 ♘h7 42 ♕f4 ♕e1+ 43 ♔h2 ♖g8 44 ♕g3 ♕xb4 45 ♘d3 ♕a3 46 ♘f4 ♕xg3+ 47 ♔xg3 ♖d8 48 ♘g6+ ♔g8 49 ♘e7+ ♔h8 50 ♘g6+ ♔g8 51

♘e7+ ♚h8 52 ♘g6+ ½-½

After 5 a4 Black can simply play 5...e6, aiming to put a bishop on the hole on b4, but this leads more to a Semi-Slav type of position, so for Slav devotees, I offer a few other ideas:

a) 5...g6 is interesting, leading to a sort of Schlecter Slav (see Chapter 11).

b) 5...♕c7 is not as stupid as it seems: Black defends b7 in advance. If 6 ♘f3 then 6...♗g4 7 ♕b3 ♗xf3 8 gxf3 e6!

c) 5...♖a7!? with the same idea. If 6 a5 then maybe 6...♗e6!? 7 ♘f3 (7 ♕b3 dxc4!) 7...dxc4 8 ♘g5 ♗g4 9 f3 ♗h5 with a completely unclear position.

Summary

In general Black is doing fine in these lines, but since the 4...a6 Slav is such a recent development, there is still scope for improvements for both colours. 4 ♘f3 a6 5 e3 b5 6 b3 ♗g4 7 h3 ♗xf3 8 ♕xf3 e6 9 ♗d3 ♗b4 10 ♗d2, as in Sadler-Levitt, is worth further tests, and the game Sadler-Hodgson is certainly crazy enough to be worth analysing!

1 d4 d5 2 c4 c6 3 ♘f3 ♘f6 4 ♘c3
> 4 e3 a6 *(D)*
>> 5 ♕c2 - *game 56*
>> 5 a4 - *game 57*

4...a6 5 e3 b5 6 b3
> 6 cxd5 - *game 55*

6...♗g4 *(D)* 7 h3
> 7 ♗e2 e6
>> 8 0-0 - *game 53*
>> 8 h3 - *game 54*

7...♗xf3 *(D)*
> 8 ♕xf3 - *game 51*
> 8 gxf3 - *game 52*

4...a6

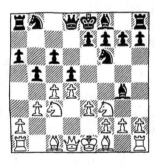

6...♗g4

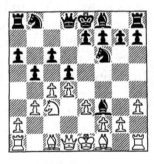

7...♗xf3

CHAPTER EIGHT

The 4...a6 Slav: Aggressive options for White

1 d4 d5 2 c4 c6 3 ♘f3 ♘f6 4 ♘c3 a6

In this chapter we deal with the more attacking systems against the 4...a6 Slav, in which White delays e2-e3 in order to develop the bishop on c1 to an active square outside the pawn chain. We shall first examine 5 c5, which has virtually become the main line.

Question 1: 5 c5 looks like a beginner's move. Isn't it bad to release the tension in the centre so early?

Answer: White is aiming for a 'big clamp' on the centre: 5 c5 stops Black from breaking with ...c6-c5, and ♗f4 will prevent Black from achieving ...e7-e5. White will then either launch a queenside offensive with b2-b4, a2-a4 and b4-b5, or he will organise a central break with e2-e4. Overall, this is a very ambitious plan.

The queenside break ...b7-b6 is not great for Black, since c5xb6, ...♕xb6 leaves him with weak dark squares on c5, b6 and a5, and a backward c-pawn.

Question 2: Black can't play on the queenside, and he can't get in any of his breaks. What can he do?

Answer: ...c6-c5 is not on the agenda, but ...e7-e5 should not be im-

possible to achieve if Black can organise his pieces properly. White has closed the centre, so Black has more time to achieve his plan, as he never has to worry about a sudden central breakthrough. Moreover, Black can spare a lot more pieces than usual to prepare ...e7-e5, since he doesn't need any to defend his own centre.

Game 58
Kramnik-Shirov
Vienna 1996

1 ♘f3 d5 2 d4 c6 3 c4 ♘f6 4 ♘c3 a6 5 c5 ♗f5 6 ♕b3 ♖a7!

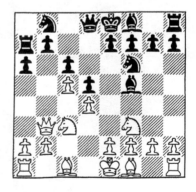

I couldn't help laughing when Julian Hodgson told me that he played ... a7-a6 in order to facilitate ...♖a7, but the idea is a good one. It really is not clear whether the queen on b3 is any better placed than the rook on a7: on b3 the queen attacks very little and gets in the way of one of White's main plans, the queenside pawn storm with b4, a4 and b5. If the queen moves away from b3, then the rook can simply return to a8!

The more conventional 6...♕c8 is discussed in the following game.

7 ♗f4 ♘bd7 8 h3 h6 9 e3 g5!

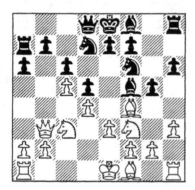

This move shows a good understanding of the position. Black leaves his weakened queenside alone and grabs space on the kingside, where White has little going for him. The move ...g7-g5 also allows the bishop to come to g7, supporting the ...e7-e5 break.

10 ♗h2 ♗g7 11 ♘e5 0-0 12 f3

Unwilling to let Black have things his own way, White prepares the e2-e4 break. This raises the stakes, as ...e7-e5 will become doubly effective against an expanded white centre.

12...♘xe5 13 ♗xe5 ♘d7 14 ♗xg7 ♔xg7 15 e4 dxe4 16 fxe4 ♗g6 17 0-0-0?

A careless move that condemns

White positionally. White had to anticipate ...e7-e5 and either prevent it with 17 e5 or play 17 ♕c4, intending 17...e5 18 d5.

17...e5! 18 ♕c4 ♕f6 19 dxe5 ♘xe5

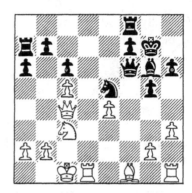

The position is now horrible for White: Black can just gang up on his weak pawns.

20 ♕d4 ♖aa8!

Having done its job, the rook comes back into play.

21 ♕e3 ♖ad8 22 ♗e2 ♕e7 23 ♖he1 ♘d7 24 ♕d4+ ♘f6 25 ♕e3 ♕e5 26 ♗f3 h5!

Preparing ...g5-g4, driving away a defender of e4.

27 a3 ♖fe8 28 ♖xd8 ♖xd8 29 ♗d1 ♖d4 30 ♗c2 ♖c4 31 ♔b1

31...♖xc5

The first pawn falls...

32 ♕d2 ♖c4 33 ♕d8 ♘xe4 34 ♗xe4 ♗xe4+ 35 ♘xe4 ♖xe4

...and now the second.

0-1

A really good exposition of the ideas behind the 4...a6 Slav.

Game 59
I.Sokolov-Shirov
Erevan Olympiad 1996

1 d4 d5 2 c4 c6 3 ♘f3 ♘f6 4 ♘c3 a6 5 c5 ♗f5 6 ♕b3 ♕c8!?

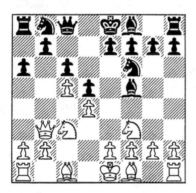

I'm not sure why Shirov did not want to repeat his previous game. Perhaps it was nothing objective, just the desire not to be too predictable. The idea behind this move is extremely neat: Black will develop normally with ...e7-e6, ...♘bd7, ...♗e7 and ...0-0, and will then prepare ...e6-e5 by means of ...♖e8 and ...♗d8-c7, making use of the fact that the queen has vacated d8!

7 ♗f4 ♘bd7 8 h3!?

Black is going to castle kingside, so White wants to have his pawn storm ready on that side of the board.

8...e6 9 ♘e5 ♗e7 10 g4 ♗g6 11 e3 ♗d8 12 ♗e2 ♘xe5 13 ♗xe5 ♗c7 14 ♘a4

This is a normal plan, trying to gain the two bishops by exchanging the knight for the dark-squared bishop on d8. However, there is a tactical problem on this occasion.

14...♗a5+! 15 ♘c3

Or 15 ♔f1 ♘e4 16 ♔g2 f6, intending ...e6-e5.

15...0-0 16 h4 h6 17 0-0-0 ♘d7 18 ♗d6 ♖e8 19 ♖hg1 ♗c7 20 h5 ♗h7 21 g5 ♗xd6 22 cxd6 ♔h8

I think that Black is just better here: White is having to make all sort of positional concessions and his attack just isn't getting anywhere.

23 gxh6 gxh6 24 e4 dxe4 25 ♘a4
♕d8 26 ♘c5 ♘xc5 27 dxc5 ♕f6 28
♕c3 ♕xc3+ 29 bxc3 ♖ab8 30 ♖d4
a5 31 ♗d1 b6 32 cxb6 ♖xb6 33
♗c2 ♖d8 34 d7 ♖b5 35 ♖gd1 ♖xh5

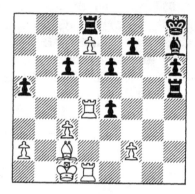

Black wins yet another pawn.
Though Sokolov fights hard, the result is never in doubt.

36 c4 ♔g7 37 ♔b2 ♔f8 38 ♗a4
♖c5 39 ♔c3 ♔e7 40 ♖d6 e3 41
fxe3 ♗e4 42 ♖6d4 ♖e5 43 ♖f1 ♗g2
44 ♖g1 ♖xe3+ 45 ♖d3 ♖xd3+ 46
♔xd3 ♖xd7+ 47 ♔e3 ♗h3 48 ♗xc6
♖c7 49 ♗b5 e5 50 ♖h1 ♗e6 51
♔d3

51...♔f6 52 ♖xh6+ ♔g5 53 ♖h8
♔f4 54 ♖h4+ ♔g4 55 ♖h8 f5 56
♖e8 ♖c5 57 a4 ♔f3 58 ♗a6 ♔f2 59

♗b5 ♗e2+ 60 ♔c3 f4 61 ♖d8 ♗f3
62 ♖d2+ ♔e1 0-1

Obviously Black is rather happier
than White in this line at the moment!

Another very popular idea for
White is to play 5 a4.

Question 4: What is the point of
this move?

Answer: 5 a4 merely aims to prevent Black's idea of ...b7-b5, and force
him to find another plan. Though it
severely weakens the b4-square, this
move does give White the possibility
of a4-a5, cramping the black queenside.

> *Game 60*
> **Pushkov-Epishin**
> *Russian Championship 1995*

1 ♘f3 ♘f6 2 c4 c6 3 ♘c3 d5 4 d4
a6 5 a4 e6

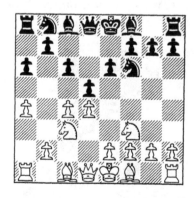

The most natural and overwhelm-
ingly the most popular choice. The
game loses a little of its Slav character
I'm afraid, but Black does get to occupy that weak b4-square.

6 ♗g5

The fianchetto 6 g3 is dealt with in the following game.

6...♘bd7 7 e3 ♗e7 8 ♗d3 0-0 9 0-0 dxc4 10 ♗xc4 c5 11 a5 cxd4 12 exd4 b5 13 axb6 ♘xb6

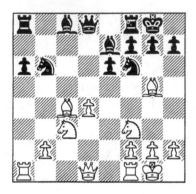

Black has already equalised.

14 ♗e2 ♗b7 15 ♘e5 h6 16 ♗h4 ♘fd7 17 ♗xe7 ♕xe7 18 ♘xd7 ♕xd7 19 ♘a4 ♘xa4 20 ♖xa4 ♖fd8 21 ♕a1 ♕c6 22 ♗f3 ♕b6 23 ♗xb7 ♕xb7 24 ♖c1 ♖d6 25 h3 ♖ad8 26 ♖cc4 e5!

Black wins a pawn, but can't quite convert it into a win.

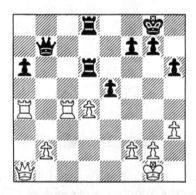

27 ♖ab4 ♕e4 28 d5 ♕xd5 29 ♕a3 ♖g6 30 ♖g4 ♖dd6 31 ♖b8+ ♔h7 32 ♕b3 ♕xb3 33 ♖xb3 ♖d1+ 34 ♔h2 ♖f6 35 f3 ♖d2 36 h4 g6 37 ♖a4

♔g7 38 ♖ba3 ♖xb2 39 ♖xa6 ♖f4 40 ♖6a4 ♖xa4 41 ♖xa4 ♖d2 42 ♔g3 ♖d3 43 ♖a5 ♔f6 44 ♖a6+ ♔f5 45 ♖a7 ♔e6 46 ♖a6+ ♖d6 47 ♖a5 f5 48 ♖a8 ♔d5 49 ♔f2 ♖b6 50 ♖d8+ ♔e6 51 ♔g3 ♖b1 52 h5 gxh5 53 ♖h8 h4+ 54 ♔xh4 ♔d5 55 ♖f8 f4 56 ♖d8+ ♔e6 57 ♖e8+ ♔f6 58 ♖f8+ ♔e7 59 ♖h8 ♖g1 60 ♖h7+ ♔f6 61 ♖xh6+ ♔g7 62 ♖e6 ♖xg2 63 ♖xe5 ♔f6 64 ♖a5 ♖g1 ½-½

Let us see what happens if White opts to fianchetto.

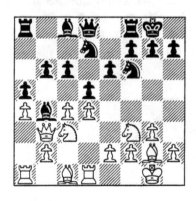

> ### Game 61
> ## Cifuentes-Dreev
> *Wijk aan Zee 1995*

1 c4 c6 2 d4 d5 3 ♘c3 ♘f6 4 ♘f3 a6 5 a4 e6 6 g3 ♘bd7 7 ♗g2 ♗b4 8 0-0 0-0 9 ♕b3 a5 10 ♖d1 b6

White will find it hard to achieve e2-e4, since Black has his bishop entrenched on b4 and can always play ....♗xc3, removing a defender of e4. Without this idea, however, White may struggle to find a plan.

11 ♘e5 ♘xe5 12 dxe5 ♘d7 13 cxd5 exd5 14 ♗f4 ♕e7 15 e4 d4! 16

♖xd4 ♘xe5 17 ♗xe5 ♕xe5

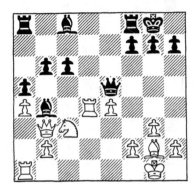

Black's two bishops and queenside pawn majority give him a clear advantage.

18 ♖d2 ♗e6 19 ♕c2 ♖ad8 20 ♖ad1 ♖xd2 21 ♖xd2 b5 22 h3 h5 23 h4 bxa4 24 ♕xa4 ♗xc3 25 bxc3 ♕xc3 26 ♖c2 ♕b4 27 ♕xc6 a4 28 ♕c3 ♕b3 29 ♔f1 ♖c8 30 ♕xb3 axb3 31 ♖d2 ♖c2 32 ♖d8+ ♔h7 33 e5 ♗f5 0-1

This does all seem fine for Black but if you cannot live happily without developing your bishop outside the pawn chain, then 5...♗f5 6 ♕b3 ♖a7 seems interesting. After 7 a5, threatening 8 ♕b6, 7...dxc4 8 ♕xc4 ♘bd7 is not so stupid. For example, 9 ♗g5 h6 10 ♗xf6 (10 ♗h4 g5!? 11 ♗g3 ♗g7 seems fine for Black) 10...exf6 (Please don't even *think* of 10...♘xf6, allowing 11 ♕c5!, winning a piece) 11 e4 ♗g4 (11...♗h7!?; 11...♗e6!?) with a very murky position.

5 ♗g5 is a sharp continuation that is only occasionally seen. White develops his bishop to its most aggressive square and is willing to sacrifice the pawn on c4 for the chance of a swift attack.

Game 62
Ward-Levitt
British Championship 1995

1 d4 d5 2 c4 c6 3 ♘c3 ♘f6 4 ♘f3 a6 5 ♗g5 dxc4

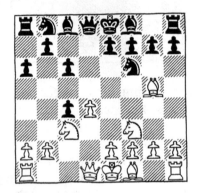

6 a4

Also possible is the immediate 6 e4!?

6...h6 7 ♗h4 ♘d5 8 e4 ♘xc3 9 bxc3 b5

Black has gone about this in a strange way. 5...♘e4 6 ♗h4 (6 h4 has been played but I don't believe it! Even 6...h6 is not stupid, when I don't see the value of h2-h4!) 6...♘xc3 7 bxc3 dxc4 8 e4 b5 is more natural if Black wants this type of position, since the omission of a2-a4 and h7-h6 must help Black a little. After 5...dxc4 6 a4 another idea is to play 6...♗f5 (a more natural Slav move), aiming for a little trap: 7 e3 ♘e4!? 8 ♘xe4 ♗xe4 9 ♗xc4 ♗xf3! 10 ♕xf3 ♕a5+! 11 ♔e2 ♕xg5 12 ♕xf7+ ♔d8, when White does not have sufficient compensation for the piece.

10 ♘e5 ♕c7 11 ♗g3 ♕b7 12 ♖b1

♕a7 13 ♕f3 e6 14 ♗e2 g6 15 ♕f6

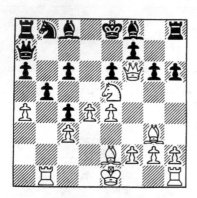

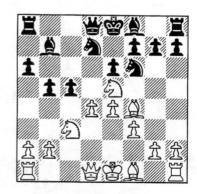

The opening has not been a success for Black, but somehow he hangs on and almost turns the tables completely.

15...♖h7 16 ♕f3 ♗b7 17 0-0 ♘d7 18 ♘xd7 ♔xd7 19 ♕f4 ♔e8 20 axb5 axb5 21 ♖a1! ♕b6 22 ♖xa8+ ♗xa8 23 ♖a1 ♕b7 24 d5 cxd5 25 exd5 ♗e7 26 ♕e3 ♗g5 27 f4 ♗e7 28 ♗f3 ♕c8 29 d6 ♗xf3 30 ♕xf3 ♕c5+ 31 ♗f2 ♕xd6 32 ♖a8+ ♗d8 33 ♖a7 ♕d5 34 ♕xd5 exd5 35 ♖b7 h5 36 ♖xb5 f5 37 ♖xd5 ♖d7 38 ♖e5+ ♔f7 39 g3 ♗f6 40 ♖c5 ½-½

Next, the adventurous 5 ♘e5. I don't like this move at all for White and in the next game Shirov neutralises it very easily with simple development.

> ### Game 63
> ### Beliavsky-Shirov
> *Erevan Olympiad 1996*

1 d4 d5 2 c4 c6 3 ♘f3 ♘f6 4 ♘c3 a6 5 ♘e5 ♘bd7 6 ♗f4 dxc4! 7 ♘xc4 b5 8 ♘e5 ♗b7 9 e4 e6 10 f3 c5!

After this freeing break, Black has no problems.

11 ♘xd7 ♘xd7 12 ♗e3 ♗e7 13 dxc5 ♘xc5 14 ♕xd8+ ♖xd8 15 ♖d1 0-0 16 a3 ♖xd1+ 17 ♔xd1 ♖c8 18 ♗e2 ♔f8 19 ♔c2 ♘a4 20 ♗d2 ♗d6 21 h3 ♔e7 22 ♖d1 ♘xc3 23 ♗xc3 b4 24 axb4 ♗xb4 25 ♖d3 a5 26 ♔b3 ♗xc3 27 ♖xc3 ♖xc3+ 28 ♔xc3 ♔d6

You might have expected the players to have called it a day here, especially when you consider that this was the last round of a gruelling Olympiad for both players: Beliavsky was playing his 14th game on board 1 and Shirov his 13th!

29 ♔d4 e5+ 30 ♔c3 ♔c5 31 ♗c4 f6

32 h4 ♗c6 33 ♗g8 h6 34 ♗c4 ♗d7
35 h5 f5 36 exf5 ♗xf5 37 ♗d3 ♗e6
38 ♗e4 ♗f7 39 g4 ♗c4 40 ♗b7
♗b5 41 ♗a8 ♗c4 42 ♗e4 ♗d5 43
♗xd5 ♔xd5 44 b3 e4 45 f4 e3 46
♔d3 e2 47 ♔xe2 ♔e4 48 g5 ♔xf4
49 gxh6 gxh6 50 ♔d3 ♔g4 51 ♔c4
♔xh5 52 ♔b5 ♔g4 53 ♔xa5 h5 54
b4 h4 55 b5 h3 56 b6 h2 57 b7
h1♕ 58 b8♕ ♕a1+ 59 ♔b6 ♕b1+
60 ♔c7 ♕xb8+ 61 ♔xb8 ½-½

In the end even these two battlers
cannot continue the game! A really
impressive display of fighting spirit
from both players.

The final idea to be considered is 5
♕b3, preventing the development of
the light-squared bishop by attacking
b7. The advantage of this move is that
Black cannot counter in normal Slav
fashion, but the Semi-Slav approach is
easy to understand, and nice for
Black.

Game 64
Lautier-Bareev
Linares 1994

**1 d4 d5 2 c4 c6 3 ♘f3 ♘f6 4 ♘c3
a6 5 ♕b3 e6**

The most popular move for Black.
5...dxc4 6 ♕xc4 ♗f5 7 g3 is the 4 ♕b3
dxc4 5 ♕xc4 ♗f5 line with the extra
moves 4 ♘c3 a6, which favour White
more than Black, while 5...♖a7 6 ♗f4!
is awkward. I briefly considered 5...b5
6 cxd5 cxd5 7 a4 b4!? 8 ♕xb4 ♘c6 9
♕b3 ♖b8 10 ♕d1 ♗f5, intending
...♘c6-b4, but 11 ♘h4 chases away
the bishop and just leaves White a
pawn up.

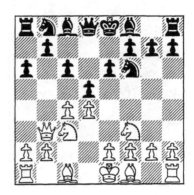

6 ♗g5?!

6 cxd5 cxd5 7 ♗g5 ♗e7 8 e3 h6 9
♗xf6 ♗xf6 10 ♗d3 ♘c6 11 0-0 0-0 12
♖ac1 was played in Piket-Shirov,
Aruba 1995, and now Shirov suggests
12...♗d7, as 13 ♕xb7 ♘a5 14 ♕b4
♗e7 snares the queen.

**6...dxc4 7 ♕xc4 b5 8 ♕d3 c5 9 a4
cxd4! 10 ♘xd4 b4 11 ♘e4 ♗b7 12
♗xf6 gxf6 13 ♖d1 ♗e7 14 ♕f3 b3!**

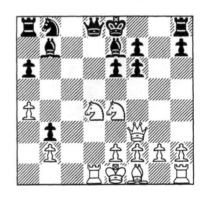

To meet 15 ♘xe6 with 15...♕a5+!
15 e3 ♕a5+ 16 ♔e2

Watch this king!
**16...♔f8 17 ♕f4 ♕e5 18 f3 ♕xf4
19 exf4 ♔g7 20 f5 ♘c6 21 fxe6
♘xd4+ 22 ♖xd4 ♖hd8 23 ♖d7 ♖xd7
24 exd7 ♖d8 25 ♔e3 f5 26 ♘g3
♗c5+ 27 ♔f4!**

g4xf5-f6-f7-f8-g8!!

27...♗d6+ 28 ♔xf5 ♖xd7 29 ♘e4 ♗c7 30 ♗c4 ♖e7 31 ♘c3 ♖e5+ 32 ♔g4 ♔h6 33 f4 ♖e3 34 ♗d5 f5+ 35 ♔xf5 ♗c8+ 36 ♔f6 ♗xf4 37 ♗xb3 ♗g5+ 38 ♔f7 ♗g4 39 ♔f8!! ♗e7+ 40 ♔g8!!

The white king completes a remarkable journey: ♔e2-e3-f4xf5-

40...♗b4 41 ♗f7 ♗xc3 42 bxc3 ♖xc3 43 ♖e1 ♖c2 44 ♗d5 ♖d2 45 ♗e4 ♗h5 46 ♖f1 ♗g6 47 ♗b7 ♖d4 48 a5 ♖a4 49 ♖f6 ♖xa5 50 ♖xa6 ♖h5 51 h3 ♖e5 52 ♖a8 ♔g5 53 ♗f3 h5 ½-½

A brilliant game!

Summary

If you had asked me a few months ago, I would have told you that Black had a few problems in the 4...a6 Slav, but now I am not so sure! 5 c5 should be avoided for the time being, while 5 a4, 5 ♘e5 and 5 ♕b3 don't really seem to promise a great deal, though 5 a4 and 5 ♕b3 can be good weapons if you know that your opponent does not like to play systems with ...e7-e6. 5 ♗g5 is aggressive and deserves further tests.

1 d4 d5 2 c4 c6 3 ♘f3 ♘f6 4 ♘c3 a6

5 c5 *(D)*

    5 a4 e6 *(D)*

        6 ♗g5 - *game 60*

        6 g3 - *game 61*

    5 ♗g5 - *game 62*

    5 ♘e5 - *game 63*

    5 ♕b3 - *game 64*

5...♗f5 6 ♕b3 *(D)*

    6...♖a7 - *game 58*

    6...♕c8 - *game 59*

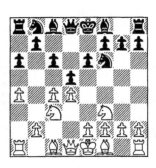

     5 c5   *5...e6*   *6 ♕b3*

CHAPTER NINE

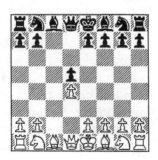

The Exchange Variation

1 d4 d5 2 c4 c6 3 cxd5 cxd5

The Exchange variation is often dismissed as just a dead draw, but several top players, Yusupov and Vaiser in particular, play it to win. What do they see in this variation?

Although the pawn structure is symmetrical, there is the open c-file to play with and we know from experience the annoying pressure that White can exert on b7. White also has the advantage of moving first in this position. Indeed, if Black does not know what he is doing, his position can very easily become highly unpleasant.

Question 1: What plans has Black tried in this position?

Answer: Black has tried two approaches:

a) To put the bishop on c8 outside the pawn chain, on either f5 or g4.

b) To unbalance the pawn structure with ...♘e4xc3.

Question 2: And what does White do?

Answer: White also has two ideas: He can put his king's knight on either f3 or e2 (after ♗d3).

Question 3: What is the difference between them?

Answer:

a) ♘f3 allows White to increase his pressure on the c-file by playing ♘e5, attacking a black knight on c6. If Black exchanges knights with ...♘xe5, then White has removed the main barrier to invasion on the c-file.

b) With ♗d3 and ♘ge2 White aims, not to attack on the c-file, but rather to keep Black passive by preventing the light-squared bishop from developing outside the pawn chain. The white bishop on d3 controls f5, while the absence of a knight from f3 means that ...♗g4 can be met by f2-f3.

> *Game 65*
> **Milov-Sadler**
> *Isle of Man 1994*

1 d4 d5 2 c4 c6 3 cxd5 cxd5 4 ♗f4

White must be wary of move-orders here as 4 ♘c3 e5!? 5 dxe5 d4 6 ♘e4 ♘c6 7 ♘f3 ♗f5 8 ♘g3 ♗g6 9 a3 ♗c5 10 ♕b3 ♘ge7, as in Tozer-Levitt, London (Lloyds Bank) 1993, gives Black good counterplay for the pawn. **4...♘c6 5 e3 ♘f6 6 ♘c3**

White could try 6 ♗d3!? here to prevent 6...♗f5. Black's best is 6...♗g4 7 ♘e2 ♗h5!, intending ...♗g6 to swap off bishops. 7 ♕b3 ♘a5! 8 ♗b5+ ♗d7 also poses few problems.

6...♗f5

The old main line. The modern 6...a6 is considered in the next game.

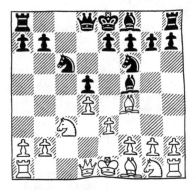

7 ♗b5 e6 8 ♘f3

4 ♘f3 ♘f6 5 ♘c3 ♘c6 6 ♗f4 ♗f5 7 e3 e6 8 ♗b5 is the normal way to reach this position. White is threatening ♘e5, ganging up on the knight on c6.

8...♘d7

Breaking the pin on the knight and thus dealing with the annoying threat of ♘e5.

9 0-0 ♗e7 10 ♕b3 g5!?

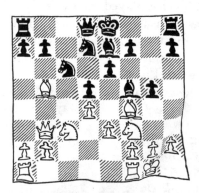

Bold but probably not the best. 10...♖c8 11 ♗xc6 bxc6 12 ♕b7 a5 is

the main line, which does not seem bad for Black, but at the board I got a little carried away. The positional idea is correct: since White has released the tension in the centre very early, Black feels much more able to take action on the wings. Indeed this idea was seen to great effect in Kramnik-Shirov from Chapter 8, but in this case White has the open c-file to help his queenside play.

11 ♗g3 h5 12 h3 g4 13 hxg4 hxg4 14 ♘d2 ♗h4 15 ♘e2 ♕a5!?

So far so good. With my last move, attacking the knight on d2, I was hoping for the reply 16 ♖fd1, when 16...♗c2! 17 ♕xc2 ♕xb5 is reasonable for Black.

16 e4!!

After a great deal of thought, my opponent found a very strong idea, blowing the centre open.

16...♕xd2 17 exf5 ♗xg3 18 ♘xg3 ♕xd4 19 ♖fe1 ♔d8 20 fxe6 fxe6 21 ♖xe6

Well, this is not great for Black, but at least I'm still alive! My opponent was already in serious time-trouble, and after the game I was really upset that I had made things so easy for him in the rest of the game.

21...♔c7 **22 ♖d1 ♘c5 23 ♖xd4 ♘xb3 24 ♖xd5 ♘bd4 25 ♖e4 ♘xb5 26 ♖xb5 ♖ad8 27 ♖e1 ♖d2 28 ♘e4 ♖e8 29 ♖e3 ♖c2 30 a4 ♖e7 31 ♘f6 ♖xe3 32 ♘d5+ ♔c8 33 ♘xe3 ♖d2 34 ♘xg4 ♖d4 35 ♘e5 ♖xa4 36 ♘xc6 bxc6 37 ♖b3 ♔c7 38 f3 c5 39 ♔f2 ♔c6 40 g4 c4 41 ♖b8 a5 42 ♔e3 ♔c7 43 ♖b5 ♔c6 44 ♖b8 ♔c7 45 ♖a8 ♖a2 46 g5 ♔b7 47 g6! c3 48 g7 c2**

Everything else is also hopeless, e.g. 48...cxb2 49 ♖b8+ ♔xb8 50 g8♕+ ♔a7 51 ♕xa2 and wins.

49 ♔d2 1-0

Now let us take a look at the fashionable 6...a6.

Game 66
Hodgson-Sadler
Ischia 1996

---

1 c4 c6 2 ♘f3 d5 3 cxd5 cxd5 4 d4 ♘f6 5 ♘c3 ♘c6 6 ♗f4 a6

The modern main line, which will be of particular interest to 4...a6 Slav players, as this line can occur by transposition after 3 ♘f3 ♘f6 4 ♘c3

a6 5 cxd5 cxd5 6 ♗f4 ♘c6.

Question 4: Why is ...a7-a6 useful in this position?

Answer: 6...a6 is a constructive waiting move: Black keeps the white pieces from occupying the b5 square, which means he no longer has to worry about ♗b5, pinning his knight on c6.

Question 5: What if White just plays 7 e3?

Answer: Then Black plays 7...♗g4 8 h3 ♗xf3 9 ♕xf3 e6. This is another example of Black giving up his light-squared bishop for White's king's knight in the Slav. In this case, since White has played cxd5 so early, Black has been able to play his knight to c6, its most natural and best square. The manoeuvre ...♗g4xf3 also removes the attacking idea ♘e5.

Question 6: So what does White do?

Answer: The only way that White can go for advantage is to avoid playing e2-e3 too early and thus sidestep ...♗xf3.

7 ♘e5!? e6

Black does not fear 8 ♘xc6 bxc6, as White is not sufficiently active to prevent Black from freeing himself with

...c6-c5.

8 e3 ♘xe5 9 ♗xe5 ♗d7!

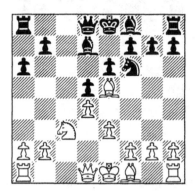

An important new idea. 9...b5 was also possible, but that does give White a bit of a target to attack on the queenside. 9...♗d7 develops the bishop to the a8-h1 diagonal (preventing White from ever achieving e3-e4), while still allowing Black to cover the c5-square with the advance ...b7-b6 if necessary.

10 ♗d3 ♗c6 11 ♕f3 ♘d7 12 ♗g3 ½-½

A real no-holds-barred classic! In mitigation, England were playing Switzerland that day in 'Euro 96' so we did have other things on our minds. (Although after watching the match for half an hour we began to think that even our game might have been more exciting!)

Game 67
Andersson-Epishin
Ter Apel 1995

1 ♘f3 ♘f6 2 c4 c6 3 d4 d5 4 cxd5 cxd5 5 ♘c3 ♘c6 6 ♗f4 a6 7 ♖c1

Here we see another attempt to delay e2-e3.

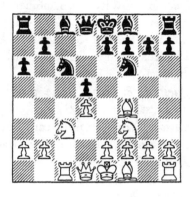

7...♗f5

7...♗g4 8 ♘e5! (the point) is annoying, but now 8 ♘e5 is met by 8...♖c8.

8 e3 e6 9 ♘e5 ♘xe5 10 ♗xe5 ♘d7 11 ♗g3 ♖c8 12 ♗d3 ♗xd3 13 ♕xd3 ♗e7 14 0-0 0-0 15 ♖c2 ♕a5 ½-½

Despairing of making anything against this plan of ...♗g4xf3, white players turned to 'Plan B': ♗d3 and ♘e2.

Game 68
Yusupov-Shirov
Zurich 1994

1 d4 d5 2 c4 c6 3 ♘c3 ♘f6 4 cxd5 cxd5 5 ♗f4 ♘c6 6 e3 ♗g4

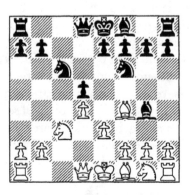

Question 7: Why not 6...a6 here?

Answer: After 6...a6 White can play 7 ♗d3 ♗g4 8 ♘ge2 (but not 8 f3 ♗h5 and Black can exchange bishops with...♗g6).

Question 8: What's the problem? Can't I just go 8...♗xe2?

Answer: You certainly can, but in comparison with the line 6 ♘f3 a6 7 e3 ♗g4 8 h3 ♗xf3 9 ♕xf3, we see that Black has an inferior version: White has played ♗d3 instead of h2-h3, and his queen is better placed on e2 than on f3. This position is perfectly playable for Black, but there just seems no point in going in for a worse version of something if there is no real need to.

Question 9: What is the point of the 6...♗g4 7 f3 ♗d7 manoeuvre?

Answer: By forcing f2-f3, Black weakens a dark square on e3 in White's position. Moreover, Black has more chance of achieving the ...e7-e5 break, since the white knight can no longer go to f3. Finally, the bishop is not too badly placed on d7, as it supports Black's counterplay with ...b7-b5.

Question 10: Wait a minute, if I get this via a transposition from the ...a7-a6 Slav, then I won't be able to play it in this way will I?

Answer: Don't worry! White can't use this subtle move-order if he transposes to the Exchange variation via the 4...a6 Slav, since he will either have shut in his dark-squared bishop (3 ♘c3 ♘f6 4 e3 a6) or will have already committed his knight to f3 (3 ♘f3 ♘f6 4 ♘c3 a6).

7 f3 ♗d7 8 ♗d3 e6

Also playable is 8...g6!?, intending 9...♗g7 to support the ...e7-e5 break.

9 ♗g3

The aggressive 9 g4 is considered in the next game, while 9 ♘ge2 allows Black to win the bishop pair with 9...♘h5.

9...♗e7 10 ♘ge2 0-0 11 0-0 a6

Black's main counterplay is to expand on the queenside, placing his knight on the c4 outpost and advancing the a- and b-pawns.

12 ♘c1!? ♘a5 13 ♘b3!

An imaginative idea: on b3, the knight protects d4, allowing White to expand in the centre with e3-e4, while eyeing the c5-square, which will be weakened by ...b7-b5. The one problem is that the knight will be in the line of fire when Black plays ...a6-a5-a4.

13...♘c4 14 ♕e2 ♖c8 15 e4 b5 16 e5 ♘h5! 17 f4 ♘xg3 18 hxg3 a5 19 ♗xh7+ ♔xh7 20 ♕h5+ ♔g8 21 ♔f2 f5 ½-½

After 22 ♖h1 White will force perpetual with ♕h8+ and ♕h5+.

Game 69
Vaiser-Nalbandian
Erevan Open 1996

1 d4 d5 2 c4 c6 3 ♘c3 ♘f6 4 cxd5 cxd5 5 ♗f4 ♘c6 6 e3 ♗g4 7 f3 ♗d7 8 ♗d3 e6 9 g4

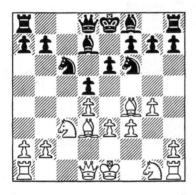

This aggressive thrust is Vaiser's trademark: White advances on the kingside, while Black counter-attacks on the queenside.

9...a6

9...♗b4 is interesting, so that after 10 a3 ♗a5 11 b4, the bishop returns to c7 and supports the central break ...e6-e5.

10 ♖c1 h6 11 h4 ♖c8 12 ♘ge2 ♘a5 13 ♔f2 ♘c4 14 ♖c2 b5 15 ♘b1 ♗c6 16 ♕c1 ♗e7 17 b3 ♘d7 18 bxc4 bxc4 19 ♗xc4 dxc4 20 ♖xc4

Although White's position is a little loose, his extra pawn will count in the end.

20...♕b6 21 ♘d2 0-0 22 g5 h5 23 ♕c3 a5 24 a3 ♗b7 25 ♖b1 ♕a6 26 ♖c7 ♗c6 27 ♖c1 ♖xc7 28 ♗xc7 ♗b5 29 ♘g3 ♖c8 30 ♕b2 g6 31 ♘ge4 a4 32 ♖c3 ♗c6 33 ♗g3 ♗d5 34 ♖xc8+ ♕xc8 35 ♘c3 ♗c6 36 e4 ♕a6

37 d5 ♗c5+ 38 ♔g2 exd5 39 exd5 ♗xd5 40 ♘de4 ♗xe4 41 ♘xe4 ♗f8 42 ♕d4 ♕e2+ 43 ♗f2 f5 44 gxf6 ♕b5 45 ♘g5 ♘e5 46 ♕e4 ♗h6 47 f7+ 1-0

Finally, we take a look at the most recent attempt from Black, 6...♘e4.

This game brought the whole idea to popular attention.

> ## Game 70
> ### Portisch-Kramnik
> *Biel Interzonal 1993*

1 d4 d5 2 c4 c6 3 cxd5 cxd5 4 ♘f3 ♘f6 5 ♘c3 ♘c6 6 ♗f4 ♘e4!?

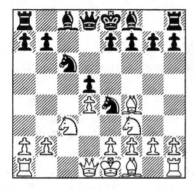

An idea of Iosif Dorfman.

Question 11: What is the point of the ...♘e4xc3 manoeuvre?

Answer: With ...♘e4xc3, Black closes the c-file, blocking one of White's major assets. Moreover, he unbalances the pawn structure, isolating the white a-pawn but giving White the chance to play a pawn to c4 for the second time!

Question 12: What if White had played one of the subtle move-orders, such as 3 cxd5 cxd5 4 ♗f4 ♘c6 5 e3 ♘f6 6 ♘c3?

Answer: Well, 6...♘e4 is still possible and leads to unclear play after 7 ♘xe4 (or 7 ♘ge2!?, intending f2-f3 to recapture on c3 with a knight) 7...dxe4, intending a quick ...e7-e5 and ...♗b4+.

7 e3 ♘xc3 8 bxc3 g6!

The key to this concept. Black anticipates that the centre will open with c3-c4 or e3-e4, and places his bishop on an influential diagonal.

9 ♗e2

9 c4 ♗g7 10 cxd5 ♕xd5 is a position from the 4 ♗g5 Grünfeld (1 d4 ♘f6 2 c4 g6 3 ♘c3 d5 4 ♗g5 ♘e4 5 ♗f4 ♘xc3 6 bxc3 ♗g7 7 e3 c5 8 cxd5 cxd4 9 cxd4 ♕xd5, etc.), which is fine for Black, while Kramnik shows that 9 ♗d3 ♗g7 10 0-0 0-0 11 e4 ♗g4 12 h3 ♗xf3 13 ♕xf3 e5! 14 dxe5 (14 exd5 ♘xd4! 15 cxd4 exf4 equalises) 14...d4!, intending ...♘xe5, is also fine. Finally, 9 ♘e5 is dealt with in the next game.

9...♗g7 10 0-0 0-0 11 c4 dxc4 12 ♗xc4 ♗f5

Kramnik gives 12...♗g4 13 h3 ♗xf3 14 ♕xf3 e5 15 dxe5 ♗xe5 16 ♗xe5 ♗xe5 as equal: 17 ♕xb7 ♗xh2+ 18 ♔xh2 ♕h4+ 19 ♔g1 ♕xc4 keeps the balance. He also suggests 12...a6!?, intending ...b7-b5.

13 ♖c1 ♖c8 14 ♕e2 a6 15 h3?

15 d5 b5 16 ♗b3 leads to a slight advantage for White according to Kramnik.

15...♘a5 16 ♗d3 ♗xd3 17 ♕xd3 ♕d7 18 ♖c3 b5 19 ♖fc1 ♘c4

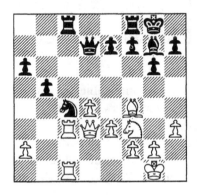

20 ♕e2 ♘b6 21 ♖c7 ♕e6 22 ♗g5 ♘d5! 23 ♖7c5 h6 24 ♗h4 b4! 25 ♕b2 ♘c3!

I like the way in which Black has moved his outpost from c4 to c3!

26 ♖xc8 ♖xc8 27 ♔h1

27 ♕xb4 ♘e2+ wins.

27...♔h7! 28 ♖a1

Or 28 ♕xb4 ♘xa2!

28...a5 29 ♕b3 ♕xb3 30 axb3 g5 31 ♗g3 a4

see following diagram

32 ♘d2 a3 33 ♖c1 e5 34 d5 a2 35 ♖a1 e4 36 d6 ♖a8 37 ♘c4 ♘b5 38 ♗e5 ♘xd6 39 ♖xa2 ♖xa2 40 ♗xd6 ♖xf2 41 ♗xb4 ♖f1+ 42 ♔h2 ♖b1 0-1

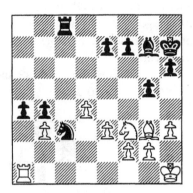

A very impressive demonstration of Black's strategy.

> ## Game 71
> ### Cifuentes-Leyva
> *Cienfuegos 1996*

1 d4 c5 2 c3 cxd4 3 cxd4 d5 4 ♘f3 ♘c6 5 ♘c3 ♘f6 6 ♗f4 ♘e4

After a weird transposition, we are back to the main position.

7 e3 ♘xc3 8 bxc3 g6 9 ♘e5 ♗g7?

A careless error. As Lalic has shown, Black can equalise with 9...♕a5! 10 ♕b3 ♗g7 11 ♗b5 ♗xe5! 12 ♗xe5 0-0.

10 ♘xc6 bxc6 11 ♕a4!

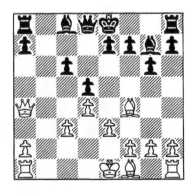

A very awkward move: Black

suddenly finds himself in big trouble. This is a good illustration of what can happen to Black if he does not take enough care.

11...♗d7 12 ♗a6! c5 13 ♕a3 cxd4 14 cxd4 0-0 15 0-0 ♗c8

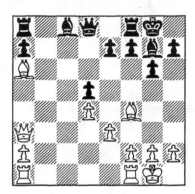

Black has to shed a pawn to meet the threat of ♗b7, winning the exchange.

16 ♗xc8 ♖xc8 17 ♕xa7 f6 18 a4 e5 19 ♗g3 ♖a8 20 ♕c5 ♖a5 21 ♕c3

♖e8 22 ♕b3 ♕b8 23 ♕a2 ♔h8 24 ♖fd1 ♕a8 25 h4 h5 26 ♖dc1 exd4 27 exd4 ♖e4 28 ♕c2 ♔h7 29 ♖d1 ♕a7 30 ♗c7 ♖a6 31 a5 ♖xd4

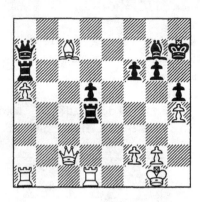

32 ♗b6

Now the inevitable advance of the white a-pawn swiftly proves to be decisive.

32...♖xd1+ 33 ♖xd1 ♕b7 34 ♕c5 ♖a8 35 ♕xd5 ♕xd5 36 ♖xd5 f5 37 ♖d8 ♖a6 38 ♖d7 ♔g8 39 ♖a7 1-0

Summary

All three major continuations of the Exchange variation seem to be doing fine for Black. Personally I would recommend either 6...a6 or 6...♗f5, as 6...♘e4 leads to positions that are more typical of the Grünfeld than the Slav.

1 d4 d5 2 c4 c6 3 cxd5 cxd5

4 ♗f4 ♘c6 5 e3
>   5 ♘f3 ♘f6 6 ♘c3
>>   6...a6 *(D)*
>>>   7 ♘e5 - *game 66*
>>>   7 ♖c1 - *game 67*
>>   6...♘e4 7 e3 ♘xc3 8 bxc3 g6 *(D)*
>>>   9 ♗e2 - *game 70*
>>>   9 ♘e5 - *game 71*

5...♘f6 6 ♘c3 ♗g4
>   6...♗f5 - *game 65*

7 f3 ♗d7 8 ♗d3 e6 *(D)*
>   9 ♗g3 - *game 68*
>   9 g4 - *game 69*

6...a6   *8...g6*   *8...e6*

CHAPTER TEN

Move-Orders and Transpositions

1 d4 d5 2 c4 c6

This chapter is extremely important both for white players, and for black players who wish to play lines with ...d5xc4. Until recently, it was thought that White had no need to be too accurate with his move-order. However, due to the efforts of Ivan Sokolov, this is no longer true.

We shall first consider 3 e3. With this move White aims to remove the force from ...d5xc4 (White can simply recapture with the bishop and has no need to play a2-a4, preventing ...b7-b5), and thus to prevent Black from entering the Slav. Usually, the game continues 3...♘f6 4 e3 e6, leading to the Semi-Slav, a very interesting opening but not the one we want to play. The following game shows the way to meet 3 e3.

> Game 72
> **Krasenkov-I.Sokolov**
> *Malmo 1995*

1 d4 d5 2 c4 c6 3 e3 ♗f5!

In the introduction, I said that ...♗f5 can only be good for Black if he can defend the b-pawn with his queen. Sokolov noticed that after 4

cxd5 cxd5 5 ♕b3, 5...♕c7 is possible as 6 ♕xd5 loses to 6...♕xc1+. 3...♗f5 is not the end of the world for White, but he has only very small chances of gaining an advantage once Black has developed his queen's bishop outside the pawn chain, while White has shut his inside.

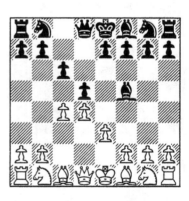

4 ♕b3 ♕c7 5 cxd5 cxd5 6 ♘c3

6 ♗b5+ is considered in the next game.

6...e6 7 ♗d2 ♘c6 8 ♘f3 ♘f6 9 ♗e2 a6 10 0-0 ♗d6 11 ♖fc1 0-0

Black has developed very naturally, and has equalised comfortably.

12 a3 ♕e7 13 ♗e1 h6

Ivan Sokolov suggests that 13...♖ad8, aiming for ...e6-e5, was most accurate.

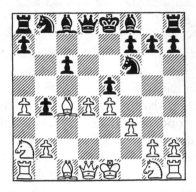

8...♕xd4 9 ♕c2

9 ♕b3, attacking f7, is strongly met by 9...♗c5! 10 ♗xf7+ ♔e7, when Black's threat of ...♕f2+ gives him an overwhelming position.

9...♗c5 10 ♗g5 ♗a6! 11 ♗b3 ♗e7 12 ♘e2 ♕b6 13 ♘g3 h6 14 ♗d2 g6 15 ♖c1 ♘fd7 16 ♘f1 ♘c5!

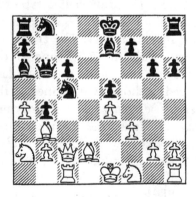

White's position is truly horrible.

17 a5 ♕b7 18 ♘xb4 ♘xb3 19 ♕xb3 c5!

This wins a piece due to the pin on the knight.

20 ♕d5 cxb4 21 ♕xe5 f6 0-1

White players will obviously not want to repeat this experience. A recent game has shown a more interest-

ing path for White.

Game 75
Hjartarson-Gulko
Reykjavik 1996

1 d4 d5 2 c4 c6 3 ♘c3 dxc4 4 e4 b5 5 a4 b4 6 ♘a2 ♘f6 7 f3 e5 8 dxe5! ♕xd1+ 9 ♔xd1 ♘fd7 10 e6!?

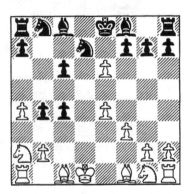

Hjartarson suggests that 10 f4 ♗a6 11 ♗e3 f6 is unclear, but 10...♘c5 may be stronger, meeting 11 ♗xc4 by 11...♗a6! 12 ♗xa6 ♘bxa6 with ideas of ...♘b3 and ...♘xa4 as well as ...♘xe4.

10...fxe6 11 ♗xc4

White has the more attractive pawn structure and hence the better long-term prospects, but Black's piece activity and the slightly open position of the white king should give him equally good chances.

11...♗a6

Also possible was 11...♘e5!?

12 ♗xa6 ♘xa6 13 ♗e3 ♗c5 14 ♔e2

see following diagram

14...0-0-0?

Hjartarson says that Black should have taken this opportunity to swap off bishops by 14...♗xe3 15 ♔xe3 0-0-0 16 ♘h3 ♘e5 17 ♖ac1 with mutual chances. In the game, Black fails to make the most of his chances and falls into an unpleasant ending.

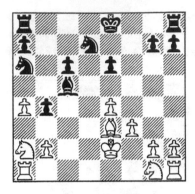

15 ♗g5! ♘f6 16 b3 ♗d4 17 ♖c1 ♔b7 18 ♘h3 e5 19 ♖hd1 c5 20 ♗e3 ♗xe3 21 ♖xd8 ♖xd8 22 ♔xe3 h6 23 ♘f2 ♖d6 24 ♖c2 ♘d7 25 ♘c1 h5 26 ♘fd3 g5 27 ♘b2 g4 28 ♘cd3! gxf3 29 gxf3 ♖g6 30 ♘c4!

White's pieces are ideally placed, and Black can no longer hold his pawn weaknesses.

30...♖g1 31 ♖b2 ♘c7 32 ♘cxe5 ♘xe5 33 ♘xe5 ♖e1+ 34 ♔f2 ♖h1 35 ♔g2 ♖c1 36 f4 ♘e6 37 f5 ♘g5 38 f6 ♔c7 39 f7 ♘h7 40 ♘g6 ♖e1

41 e5 ♔c6 42 ♔f2 ♖e4 43 ♖e2 ♖g4 44 e6 1-0

Nice technique from Hjartarson, and a critical new idea for White.

In view of Ivan Sokolov's success with 3...dxc4 against 3 ♘c3, you may be wondering whether Black can play 3...dxc4 against 3 ♘f3 but, amongst others, the following game has put the line under a cloud. It is so unbalanced, however, that I would not be at all surprised if there is a sneaky resource for Black!

> ## Game 76
> ## Miles-Hodgson
> *Hastings 1995/96*

1 ♘f3 d5 2 d4 c6 3 c4 dxc4

3 ♘f3 ♗f5 4 cxd5 cxd5 5 ♕b3 ♕c7 is tactically possible as 6 ♕xd5 allows mate after 6...♕xc1+. The crucial difference with the 3 e3 line is that White has not blocked in his dark-squared bishop, which means that after 6 ♘c3 e6, 7 ♗f4! is extremely nasty: 7...♕xf4 loses the rook on a8 after 8 ♕xb7, while 7...♕b6 8 ♕xb6 axb6 9 e3, intending ♗b5+, ♔e2 and then ♖hc1 to invade on the c-file, gives Black a very depressing ending to defend.

4 e3 b5 5 a4!

see following diagram

The main difference between 3 ♘c3 and 3 ♘f3 is that Black cannot advance his queenside pawns with tempo against 3 ♘f3. This gives White plenty of time to undermine them.

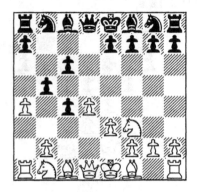

5...e6 6 axb5 cxb5 7 b3 &b4+ 8 &d2 &xd2+ 9 ♘bxd2 a5 10 bxc4 b4

A very confusing situation: Black has two passed queenside pawns while White has more central control. The essential conflict is whether Black can get his pawns moving or whether White can blockade them so that they will become weak.

11 ♘e5!

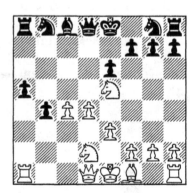

Threatening 12 ♘xf7! ♔xf7 13 ♕f3+, winning the rook on a8.

11...♘f6 12 ♕a4+!

This is the key idea, forcing Black's pieces into a nasty tangle. 12...♘bd7 loses a pawn to 13 ♘c6, while 12...&d7 13 ♘xd7 is exactly what White wants: 13...♘bxd7 14 &e2 0-0

15 0-0 ♕c7 16 &f3! (16 ♘b3? ♘e4!, aiming for c3, is to be avoided at all costs) 16...♖a7 17 c5 is very nice for White.

12...♘fd7 13 c5! 0-0 14 ♘ec4!

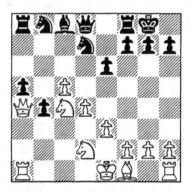

Exchanges help Black free himself.

14...♘f6 15 &e2 ♘d5 16 &f3 &d7 17 ♕c2 &b5 18 ♘d6 &a6 19 ♘2c4 ♘c6 20 0-0 ♕c7 21 ♖fc1 &xc4 22 ♘xc4 ♘ce7 23 ♕b3 ♖a7 24 g3! ♖b8 25 ♔g2!

Very instructive: Black's pawns are going nowhere, so White quietly improves his position, removing the possibility of back-rank mates and making sure that if Black does queen, it won't be with check.

25...h6 26 ♖c2 ♘c3?

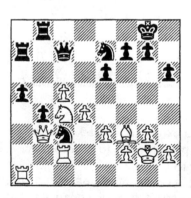

Allowing a combination, but Black was struggling to find anything to do.
27 ℤxa5! ℤxa5 28 ♘xa5 ♕xa5 29 ℤxc3 bxc3 30 ♕xb8+ ♔h7 31 ♕b7 f5 32 ♕xe7 c2 33 ♕xe6 c1♕ 34 ♕xf5+ g6 35 ♕f7+ ♔h8 36 ♕f8+ ♔h7 37 ♗d5!

Mate cannot be averted.
37...♕h1+!? 38 ♔xh1 1-0

The next line is 3 ♘f3 ♘f6 4 e3. I am surprised at how popular this variation is, as it really doesn't promise White very much at all, and his results have not really been that good.

> ## Game 77
> ### Kozul-Illescas
> *Erevan Olympiad 1996*

1 d4 d5 2 c4 c6 3 ♘f3 ♘f6 4 e3 ♗f5!

I don't think that this needs any comment!

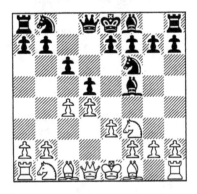

5 ♗d3

5 cxd5 cxd5 6 ♕b3 is the other way to play, leading to positions very similar to Game 72.
5...♗xd3 6 ♕xd3 e6 7 0-0 ♘bd7 8 ♘c3 ♗b4 9 ♗d2 a5 10 a3 ♗e7 11

b3 0-0 12 e4?

12...♘c5!! 13 dxc5 dxe4! 14 ♕xd8 ℤfxd8

The point: Black regains his piece with a vastly superior position, as the knight on f3 is tied to the defence of the bishop on d2.
15 ♘a4 exf3 16 ℤfd1 ℤd3 17 ♗c3 ℤad8 18 ℤe1 ℤ8d7 19 ℤac1 fxg2 20 ♘b2 ℤf3 21 ♔xg2 ℤf5 22 ♘a4 ℤd3 23 ℤcd1 ℤdf3 24 ℤe2 h5! 25 h3 g5!

This kingside advance finishes off the game.
26 b4 axb4 27 axb4 g4 28 hxg4 ♘xg4

Now f2 must fall.
29 ℤh1 ℤxf2+ 30 ℤxf2 ♘xf2 31

♖a1 h4 32 ♘b6 h3+ 33 ♔h2 ♖g5 34 ♖g1 ♖xg1 35 ♔xg1 ♘g4 36 ♘c8 ♔f8 0-1

And finally, 4 ♕b3 and 4 ♕c2. In both case White's queen protects c4 and prevents the light-squared bishop from developing safely: 4 ♕b3 attacks b7, while 4 ♕c2 covers the f5-square. However, these moves do nothing to further White's development, while exposing the white queen to attack by Black's minor pieces. Although neither line promises much, they are both popular with positional players who wish to avoid any sharp options. Recently, black players have been trying a Semi-Slav approach, 4...e6 5 g3 dxc4 6 ♕xc4 b5 7 ♕c2 ♗b7, with ...♘bd7 and ...c6-c5 to follow, but as befits a book on the Slav, I will concentrate on our beloved plan of developing the light-squared bishop outside the pawn chain.

Game 78
Akopian-Shirov
Wijk aan Zee Open 1993

---

1 d4 d5 2 ♘f3 ♘f6 3 c4 c6 4 ♕b3 dxc4

The most solid and reliable option. Black diverts the queen from its attack on b7, thereby allowing the light-squared bishop to develop to f5. I suppose that 4...a6 is possible here, as 5 ♗f4 (preventing ...♖a7!) 5...b5 6 cxd5 cxd5 7 a4 b4! 8 ♘bd2 (8 ♕xb4 e5! wins a piece) 8...♘c6 9 ♖c1 ♗b7 10 ♘e5 (to remove the knight on c6, which both guards b4 and blocks the c-file) is met by 10...♘a5! (10...♘xd4

11 ♕xb4 attacks b7 and d4) 11 ♕xb4 e6 12 ♕c3 ♖c8!, winning the queen, as 13 ♕d3 allows 13...♖xc1+ mate! Instead of 6...cxd5, 6...♘xd5!? (hitting the bishop on f4) 7 ♗g3 e6!?, intending a quick ...c6-c5, is also interesting. Note that 5 ♘c3 transposes to 4 ♘f3 a6 5 ♕b3.

5 ♕xc4 ♗f5 6 ♘c3 ♘bd7 7 g3 e6 8 ♗g2 ♗e7 9 0-0 0-0 10 e3

Be warned! The 'natural' 10 ♖d1 loses the exchange to 10...♗c2!, as 11 ♖d2 allows 11...♘b6!, trapping the queen!

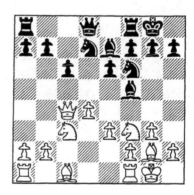

10...♘e4 11 ♕e2

A novelty. 11 ♘d2 is the old move, when theory recommends 11...♘xd2 12 ♗xd2 e5! 13 e4 cxd4 14 exf5 dxc3 15 ♗xc3 ♗f6! 16 ♖ad1?! ♗xc3 17 bxc3 ♕c7 with equality. White must consider 16 ♗b4!?, retaining the bishop pair.

11...♘xc3 12 bxc3 ♗e4!

A typical manoeuvre, preventing e3-e4 and neutralising White's bishop on g2.

13 c4 c5 14 ♖d1 ♕c7

---

see following diagram

---

15 ♗b2 ♘b6!?

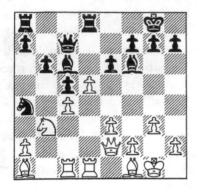

The start of an eccentric plan from Shirov. 15...罣fd8, intending 16...罣ac8 and then ...公d7-b8-c6 to pressurise c4 and d4, was also interesting.

16 罣ac1 鱼f6 17 鱼f1!

To chase the bishop from e4 without allowing the exchange of bishops.

17...公a4!? 18 鱼a1 罣fd8 19 公d2 鱼c6 20 公b3 b6 21 d5

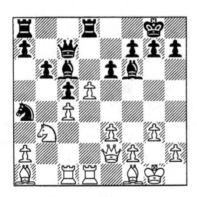

21...鱼xa1 22 dxc6 鱼f6 23 鱼g2 公c3 24 罣xd8+ 罣xd8 25 豐c2 罣d6 26 罣e1 罣xc6 27 鱼xc6 豐xc6 28 公d2 a6 29 公b1 公e4 30 h4 b5 31 cxb5 axb5 32 公d2 公c3 33 公b1 公e4 34 公d2 公c3 ½-½

I am a little surprised that White accepted the draw here. Although his opponent has good counterplay,

White is material up, after all!

Game 79
Razuvaev-Sturua
Erevan Open 1996

1 d4 公f6 2 c4 c6 3 公f3 d5 4 豐c2 g6

A very sensible idea. Black allows his bishop to develop to g7 whilst supporting ...鱼c8-f5, attacking the queen. 4...a6 5 鱼f4 b5?! 6 cxb5 cxb5 7 公bd2! (intending 公b3) is best avoided, as White's pieces are well placed to exploit the queenside dark-square weaknesses, so Black should try 5...dxc4 6 豐xc4 e6 7 e3 b5 8 豐c2 鱼b7, intending ...公b8-d7 and ...c6-c5. Finally, 4...dxc4 5 豐xc4 transposes to the previous game.

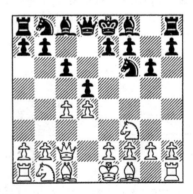

5 鱼f4 鱼g7

5...公a6!? is considered in the next game and 5...dxc4 is also good: 6 豐xc4 鱼g7 7 e3 (7 公c3 0-0 8 e4 b5 leads to a typical Grünfeld position which, though reasonable for Black, may not appeal to pure Slav players) 7...0-0 8 鱼e2 鱼e6 9 豐c1 公bd7 10 0-0 c5! 11 公c3 公d5! 12 罣d1 罣c8 13 公xd5 鱼xd5 14 dxc5 公xc5 15 鱼c4 公d3! 16

♖xd3 ♖xc4 17 ♕d2 e6 gave Black no problems in Goldin-Yusupov, Tilburg 1992. However, 5...♗f5 6 ♕b3 ♕b6 7 c5 ♕xb3 8 axb3 is a touch better for White, and not very exciting for Black.

6 e3 0-0 7 ♘c3 ♗e6

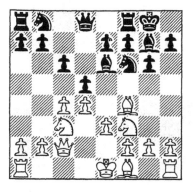

8 ♘g5

8 ♕b3 dxc4 9 ♗xc4 (9 ♕xb7 ♘d5!?, intending to trap the queen in the corner after 10 ♕xa8 ♕b6, is extremely murky but not worse for Black) 9...♗xc4 10 ♕xc4 ♘d5 11 ♗g3 ♘a6, intending ...♘d5-b6 and ...c6-c5 is about equal.

8...♗f5 9 ♕b3 ♕b6 10 ♗e2 ♘bd7 11 ♘f3

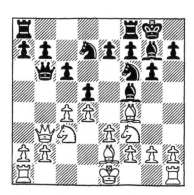

The endings with 11 c5 ♕xb3 12

axb3 are improved for Black, as the white knight is misplaced on g5, which makes ...e7-e5 easier to achieve. **11...♗g4 12 cxd5 ♘xd5 13 ♘xd5 cxd5 14 ♕xb6 ♘xb6 ½-½**

And finally, an amazing sacrificial line in this most solid of openings!

Game 80
Alburt-Shabalov
USA Championship 1996

1 d4 d5 2 c4 c6 3 ♘f3 ♘f6 4 ♕c2 g6 5 ♗f4 ♘a6!? 6 e3 ♗f5 7 ♕b3 ♘b4!!

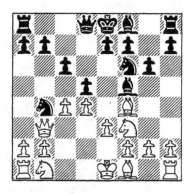

A typically inventive idea of Kupreichik.

8 ♕xb4 e5 9 ♕xb7

9 c5 exf4 10 exf4 b6 11 ♘e5 bxc5 12 ♕b7 ♗d7 13 ♘xd7 ♘xd7 14 ♕xc6 ♖c8 15 ♕xd5 cxd4 16 ♗b5 ♗b4+ (16...♖c1+ 17 ♔d2 ♖xh1 18 ♕e5+! ♕e7 19 ♕xh8+ ♕f8 20 ♕e5+ leads to a draw by repetition) gave Black a powerful initiative in Epishin-Kupreichik, Russia 1989.

9...♖b8 10 ♕xc6+ ♗d7 11 ♕xf6! ♕xf6 12 ♗xe5 ♕b6 13 b3 ♗b4+ 14 ♘bd2 0-0 15 ♗xb8 ♖xb8

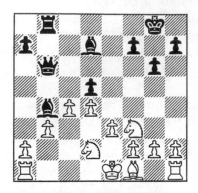

16 cxd5

A strange move to play since Shabalov had already won a convincing game in this line. 16 ♗d3 is the theoretical recommendation, meeting 16...♗g4 with 17 ♔e2 ♕a5 (threatening...♗b4xd2) 18 ♖hd1, which is a bit of a mess. 17 0-0!? seems more natural, to counter 17...♕a5 with 18 h3! ♗h5 (18...♗xd2 19 hxg4 ♗c3 20 ♖ac1 ♗b2 21 ♖c2 ♕xa2 22 ♘d2! [intending ♖b1] 22...♖xb3 23 ♘xb3 ♕xb3 24 ♖b1 ♕xd3 25 ♖cxb2 dxc4 26 ♖c1, intending ♖bc2 with an advantage) 19 a3! ♗xd2 20 b4! ♗xb4 21 axb4 ♕xb4 22 ♖ab1 ♕f8 23 g4!,

winning.

16...♕a5 17 ♗c4 ♗g4 18 0-0 ♗xd2

White has some pawns, but Black has the big guys!

19 ♘e5 ♗f5 20 a3 ♕c3 21 d6 ♔g7 22 ♘xf7 ♖b6 23 e4 ♗c8 24 ♖fd1 ♗f4 25 e5

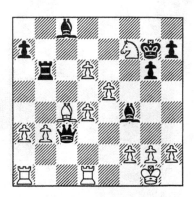

25...♖xb3 26 ♗xb3 ♕xb3 27 ♘d8 ♕b6 28 g3 ♕xd8 29 gxf4 ♕h4 30 f3 ♕xf4 31 ♔f2 ♗b7 32 ♖d3 ♗a6 33 d7 ♕xh2+ 34 ♔e3 ♕h6+ 35 ♔e2 ♕h4 36 ♔d2 ♔f7 37 d5 ♔e7 38 e6 ♕f2+ 39 ♔c3 ♕c5+ 40 ♔d2 ♗xd3 41 ♖c1 ♕d4 42 ♖c8 ♗b5+ 43 ♔c2 ♗xd7 0-1

A fascinating game.

Summary

3 e3 ♗f5 equalises for Black; 3 ♘c3 dxc4 is a very interesting line and only Hjartarson-Gulko (Game 75) is a possible attempt to play with White; 3 ♘f3 dxc4 is very unbalanced but seems to be good for White; 3 ♘f3 ♘f6 4 e3 ♗f5 is nothing for White; while 3 ♘f3 ♘f6 4 ♕c2 and 4 ♕b3 are also nothing special. Hence 3 ♘f3 ♘f6 4 ♘c3 dxc4 is the most accurate order for both sides.

1 d4 d5 2 c4 c6

3 e3

> 3 ♘c3 dxc4 4 e4 b5 5 a4 b4 6 ♘a2 ♘f6 7 f3 e5 *(D)*
>> 8 ♗xc4 - *game 74*
>> 8 dxe5 - *game 75*
>
> 3 ♘f3
>> 3...dxc4 - *game 76*
>> 3...♘f6
>>> 4 e3 ♗f5 - *game 77*
>>> 4 ♕b3 - *game 78*
>>> 4 ♕c2 g6 5 ♗f4 *(D)*
>>>> 5...♗g7 - *game 79*
>>>> 5...♘a6 - *game 80*

3...♗f5 4 ♕b3 ♕c7 5 cxd5 cxd5 *(D)*
> 6 ♘c3 - *game 72*
> 6 ♗b5+ - *game 73*

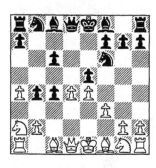
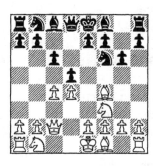

7...e5	*5 ♗f4*	*5...cxd5*

CHAPTER ELEVEN

Odds and Ends

1 d4 d5 2 c4 c6

In this chapter, we take a brief look at all the sidelines that I couldn't fit into the main chapters!

A) The Winawer Counter-Gambit: 3 ♘c3 e5

This gambit was all the rage four or five years ago, but the following game somewhat dampened the ardour of the black players.

> Game 81
> **Kasparov-Nikolic**
> *Manila Olympiad 1992*

1 d4 d5 2 c4 c6 3 ♘c3 e5 4 dxe5 d4 5 ♘e4 ♕a5+ 6 ♗d2!

This natural move had been practically ignored prior to this game (6 ♘d2 had been the main line).

6....♕xe5 7 ♘g3!

This move looks obvious, but it was Kasparov's new idea. Of course, the genius is not in the move itself, but in the astonishing attacking plan that flows from it. It is not easy to guess that White is gearing up for kingside attack!

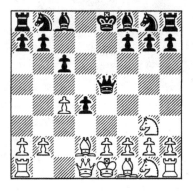

7...♕d6

Black has also tried 7...c5, but after 8 ♘f3 ♕c7 9 e3 dxe3 10 ♗xe3 ♘f6 11 ♗d3 White is slightly better due to his lead in development.
8 ♘f3 ♘f6 9 ♕c2 ♗e7 10 0-0-0! 0-0

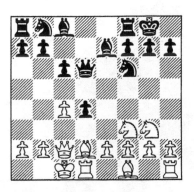

11 e3

Azmaiparashvili, a long-time analyst for Kasparov, played 11 ♗c3 against Eslon in Seville 1994. 11...dxc3!? 12 ♖xd6 cxb2+ is given as unclear by 'Gazza', but 'Azmai' claims an advantage after 13 ♕xb2 ♗xd6 14 e4 (threatening e4-e5) 14...♗f4+ 15 ♔b1. This assessment is objectively correct, as White's material advantage, coupled with the threat of e4-e5, driving away the knight on f6 and exposing the bishop on f4 to attack by White's pieces (♕b2-d4, ♘g3-h5), should tell in the end. However, in a practical game White's dark-square weaknesses and exposed king give Black definite counter-chances. Eslon played 11...♕f4+, unpinning, and White sacrificed a pawn with 12 e3 dxe3 13 fxe3 (13 ♖d4!? looks very strong, meeting 13...♕h6 with 14 ♖h4! ♕g6 15 ♗d3!, trapping the queen, and 13...♕c7 with 14 ♗d3!? or just 14 fxe3 with very dangerous attacking play) 13...♕xe3+ 14 ♔b1 ♘a6 15 ♘d4 (aiming to put a knight on f5 and threatening ♖de1, winning the bishop on e7).

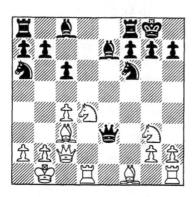

Now after 15...♗b4 16 ♘df5 ♗xf5

17 ♘xf5 ♕e6 18 ♗d3 White had a superb attacking position for the pawn. This looks very smooth and, in his annotations, Azmaiparashvili comments that if Black tries to improve with 15...♘b4 (instead of ...♗b4) then 16 ♕b3 c5 17 ♖e1 wins after 17...♕g5 18 ♖xe7 cxd4 19 ♗xb4, but in fact 16...♗c5! is extremely good for Black, as 17 ♗xb4 ♕xb3 18 ♘xb3 ♗xb4 and 17 ♖e1 ♕f4! (threatening ...♗xd4) 18 ♗xb4 ♕xd4 both leave Black simply a pawn up. The position is extremely risky for Black, of course, and I would not recommend this sort of position against a good attacking player, but Black's tactical chances must not be underestimated.

11...dxe3 12 fxe3!

This is the key to the whole idea as 12 ♗xe3 ♕c7 promises nothing for White. The text allows the bishop on d2 to move with tempo to the attacking diagonal a1-h8.

12...♕c7

12...♘a6 is considered in the next game.

13 ♗c3 ♗g4?! 14 ♗d3 ♘bd7 15 ♗f5!

Naturally, White wants to occupy

the f5-square with his knight.

15...♗xf5 16 ♘xf5 ♖fe8 17 ♘xg7!! ♔xg7 18 ♕f5 ♘f8 19 h4!

In order to chase away the knight on f8 if it should surface on g6.

19...h6 20 g4?!

20 ♕g4! ♘g6 21 h5 was even stronger according to Kasparov.

20...♕c8 21 ♕xc8 ♖axc8 22 g5!

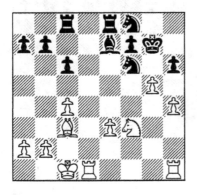

The ending is still very unpleasant for Black, and Kasparov powers through with his customary energy.

22...♘8d7 23 e4 ♖cd8 24 ♖df1 ♔f8 25 gxf6 ♗xf6 26 e5 ♗g7 27 ♖hg1 c5 28 ♔c2 ♖e6 29 ♖g4 ♗h8 30 b4 b6 31 bxc5 bxc5 32 ♖b1 ♖a6 33 ♖b2 ♗g7 34 ♖b7 ♖xa2+ 35 ♔b3 ♖a6 36 e6 ♖xe6 37 ♖xg7 1-0

If Black wishes to play this line, he needs to find an improvement on 12...♕c7.

Game 82
Rogozenko-Bets
Moldovan Championship 1994

1 d4 d5 2 c4 c6 3 ♘c3 e5 4 dxe5 d4 5 ♘e4 ♕a5+ 6 ♗d2 ♕xe5 7 ♘g3 ♘f6 8 ♘f3 ♕d6 9 ♕c2 ♗e7 10 0-0-0 0-0 11 e3 dxe3 12 fxe3

Following Kasparov's example.

12...♘a6

12...♖d8 is possible, preventing 13 ♗c3 as 13...♕xd1+ 14 ♕xd1 ♖xd1+ 15 ♔xd1 exchanges queens, destroying White's attacking possibilities.

13 ♗c3 ♕c7

Since this turns out so badly, Black must consider 13...♕e6, keeping the queen close to the kingside to help with defence, while threatening ...♘b4 and ...♘g4 as well as ...♕xe3+.

14 a3!

see following diagram

Preventing 14...♘b4, activating the knight.

14...♘g4!? 15 ♖e1 ♗f6

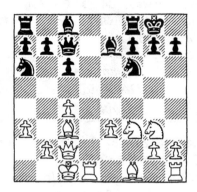

This manoeuvre, exchanging the dangerous bishop on c3, briefly gave black players hope in this line.

16 h3! ♗xc3 17 hxg4

Obviously 17...♗xe1 loses to 18 ♕xh7+ mate.

17...h6 18 ♕xc3 ♕xg3 19 g5! hxg5 20 ♗d3 ♖d8 21 ♖h7 f6 22 ♖eh1 ♕c7 23 ♘xg5 ♔f8 24 c5! ♗g4 25 ♕xf6+! 1-0

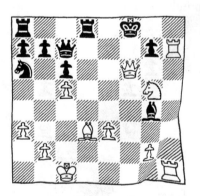

25...gxf6 26 ♖h8+ ♔e7 27 ♖1h7+ is mate!

B) **The Schlecter Slav:**
3 ♘c3 ♘f6 4 e3 g6

Question 1: What is the idea behind this system?

Answer: This is another Smyslov favourite. Black accepts a slight space disadvantage and develops his king's bishop on g7, avoiding ...e7-e6 in order to retain the option of developing his bishop on c8 outside the pawn chain if he wishes.

> ### Game 83
> ### Gulko-Salov
> *Reykjavik (World Cup) 1991*

1 ♘f3 d5 2 c4 c6 3 e3 ♘f6 4 ♘c3 g6 5 d4 ♗g7 6 ♗e2 0-0 7 0-0 b6

A solid move, developing the bishop to b7 to support Black's centre. The more active 7...dxc4 8 ♗xc4 ♗g4 is dealt with in the next game.

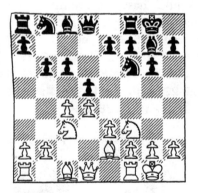

8 cxd5 cxd5 9 ♘e5!

When the central pawn structure becomes fixed, the first side to gain a central space advantage will be able to claim the initiative.

9...♗b7 10 ♗d2 ♘fd7?!

10...♘c6 was stronger, meeting 11 f4 with 11...♘e8!, intending to develop the knight to d6, when Black only stands a little worse.

11 f4! f6 12 ♘f3!?

12 ♘d3 is also possible. Black has

not developed his pieces harmoniously: the king's knight stops the queen's knight from developing to d7 and has no moves of its own.

12...♖f7 13 ♗d3 ♘f8

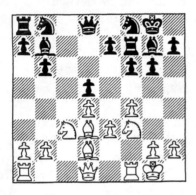

14 f5?!

A little hasty according to Gulko, who prefers 14 g4! e6 15 f5.

14...gxf5 15 ♗xf5 e6 16 ♗d3 ♘c6 17 ♘e2 ♕d6 18 ♘g3 ♘g6 19 ♘h5 ♗h8 20 ♕e2 ♖af8 21 a3 e5 22 dxe5 fxe5 23 ♘g5 ♖xf1+ 24 ♖xf1 ♗c8? 25 ♖xf8+ ♕xf8 26 ♗e4!

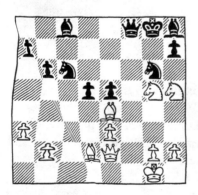

A very nice *move*. 26...dxe4 loses to 27 ♕c4+.

26...♘ce7 27 ♗b4! ♗b7 28 ♕g4 ♕c8 29 ♕f3 ♕f8 30 ♕h3 ♕c8 31 ♘f6+ ♔g7 32 ♕xh7+ ♔xf6 33

♗xe7+ ♘xe7 34 ♕h6+ ♘g6 35 ♕xg6+ ♔e7 36 ♕h7+ ♔d6 37 ♘f7+ ♔c7 38 ♗f5 1-0

Game 84
Dreev-Piket
Dortmund 1994

---

1 d4 ♘f6 2 c4 c6 3 ♘f3 d5 4 e3 g6 5 ♘c3 ♗g7 6 ♗e2

White can try 6 ♗d3 (preventing ...♗f5) 6...0-0 7 h3 (preventing ...♗g4) if he wants to prevent the plan in the game, although 7...c5 is an interesting reply. The game transposes to a quiet variation of the Grünfeld, in which White has played the useful, though hardly earth-shattering, extra move h2-h3.

6...0-0 7 0-0 dxc4!? 8 ♗xc4 ♗g4

This is a much more active idea: Black will follow up with ...♘bd7 and a quick ...e7-e5.

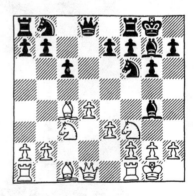

9 h3 ♗xf3 10 ♕xf3 ♘bd7 11 ♗b3

The critical line is 11 ♖d1 e5 12 d5 e4!? 13 ♘xe4 ♘xe4 14 ♕xe4 ♘b6 15 ♗b3 (threatening d5xc6; Bareev suggests 15 ♖b1!?, protecting b2 and seeking to avoid the time-loss with ♗c4-b3xd5 as in the game) 15...cxd5 16

♗xd5 ♘xd5 17 ♖xd5 ♛b6.

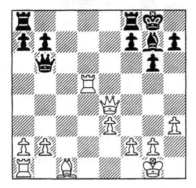

Question 2: What is going on here?

Answer: Black has sacrificed a pawn for a lead in development and pressure against the b2-pawn. However, this play is sufficient to regain the pawn, but not to achieve complete equality: 18 ♕d3 ♖ad8 19 e4! ♗d4 20 ♔h1 ♗xf2 21 ♗h6 ♖xd5 22 exd5 ♖d8 23 ♖d1 ♕d6 24 ♕c3, intending ♕g7+ mate, when White's passed d-pawn and Black's weak kingside gave White a slight advantage in Bareev-Kramnik, Novgorod 1994.

11...e5 12 ♖d1 ♕e7 13 e4?! exd4 14 ♖xd4 ♖ad8 15 ♗e3 ♘c5 16 ♗c2 ♘fd7 17 ♖dd1 b5!

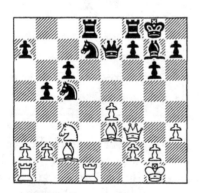

Black activates his queenside major-

ity and gains space.

18 ♕e2 ♘b6! 19 ♖xd8 ♖xd8 20 ♖e1 ♘c4!

Imperceptibly, White has drifted into big trouble: Black controls the central dark squares and White's queenside is an easy target.

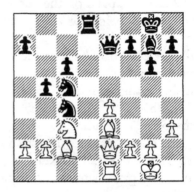

21 ♗c1 ♘e6 22 ♕f1 ♕c5 23 ♗b3 ♘d2 24 ♗xd2 ♖xd2 25 ♗xe6 fxe6 26 e5 ♖xb2 27 ♘e4 ♕xe5 28 ♕d3 ♕d5 29 ♕g3 ♗e5 30 f4 ♗d4+ 31 ♔h2 c5 32 ♕h4 ♖xa2 33 ♕e7 h5!

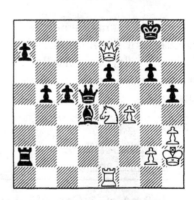

34 ♕e8+ ♔g7 35 ♕e7+ ♔h6 36 h4 ♕f5 37 ♘g3 ♕xf4 38 ♖xe6 ♖a1

Here White lost on time.

What I like about the Schlecter Slav is its flexibility: on move 7, Black has a huge range of plans. We have seen:

a) 7...b6 reinforcing the centre by fianchettoing the other bishop; and

b) 7...dxc4 8 ♗xc4 ♗g4 to break quickly in the centre by means of ...♘bd7, ...♗xf3 and ...e7-e5; but Black can also try

c) 7...a6 to expand on the queenside with ...b7-b5, before or after ...d5xc4; and

d) 7...♘e4!? to unbalance the pawn structure with ...♘xc3. Bates-Sadler, British Championship 1995, continued 8 ♕b3 b6 9 ♘xe4 (9 cxd5 ♘xc3! 10 bxc3 cxd5 intending ...♘c6-a5, hitting the queen) 9...dxe4 10 ♘d2 f5 11 f3 e5 12 dxe5 exf3! 13 ♘xf3 ♘d7, regaining the pawn with a better pawn structure;

...and the list continues! There really is huge scope for personal ideas.

C)   3 ♘f3 ♘f6 4 ♘c3 dxc4 5 e3

This was one of my favourites when I was little, but I'm not quite sure why I decided to play it against Bareev! It is actually not a very promising continuation.

> ### Game 85
> ### Sadler-Bareev
> *Hastings 1992/93*

1 d4 d5 2 c4 c6 3 ♘f3 ♘f6 4 ♘c3 dxc4 5 e3

see following diagram

Trying to manage without the standard 5 a4, which prevents the advance ...b7-b5.

5...b5 6 a4 b4 7 ♘b1

7 ♘a2, attacking the b4-pawn, regains the pawn by force, but seriously misplaces the knight. The text is more ambitious.

7...♗a6 8 ♗e2

8 ♘bd2 regains the pawn, but after 8...c3 9 bxc3 ♗xf1 10 ♘xf1 bxc3 Black will break with ...c6-c5 and equalise.

8...c5! 9 0-0 ♘c6 10 dxc5 ♘a5! 11 ♘bd2 e6 12 b3 ♗xc5 13 ♗b2 c3 14 ♗xa6 cxb2 15 ♗b5+ ♔e7

The king is very safe in the centre. Bareev rapidly outplays me, but around the time control begins to ask too much of his slight advantage.

16 ♖b1 a6 17 ♗e2 ♕b6 18 ♖xb2

♘d5 19 ♘c4 ♘xc4 20 ♗xc4 ♘c3 21 ♕c2 ♕c7 22 ♕c1 ♖hd8 23 ♖d2 a5 24 ♕c2 g6 25 ♖c1 ♗d6 26 g3 ♗e5 27 ♗f1 h5 28 ♗c4 ♕c5 29 h4 ♗f6 30 ♗f1 ♖ac8 31 ♖xd8 ♖xd8 32 ♘d2 ♖c8 33 ♘c4 g5 34 hxg5 ♕xg5 35 ♕h7 ♖h8 36 ♕d3 ♖d8 37 ♕h7 ♖h8 38 ♕d3 ♕c5 39 ♖c2 ♖d8 40 ♕h7 h4 41 gxh4 ♖h8 42 ♕d3 ♖d8 43 ♕h7 ♖h8 44 ♕d3 ♖g8+ 45 ♔g2 ♖d8 46 ♕h7 ♖h8 47 ♕d3 ♖d8 48 ♕h7 ♘xa4?

Too risky. After the tactics, Black only just manages to hold on to the draw.

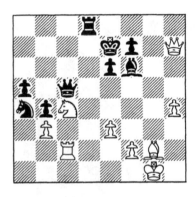

49 ♖a2! ♘b2 50 ♘xa5 ♕c1+ 51 ♔h2 ♖h8 52 ♘c6+ ♕xc6 53 ♖a7+ ♔d6 54 ♕xh8 ♗xh8 55 ♗xc6 ♔xc6 56 ♖xf7 ♘d3 57 h5 ♘c5 58 h6 ♘xb3 59 ♖f8 ♗e5+ 60 f4 ♗b2 61 e4 ♘c5 62 e5 ♘d7 63 h7 ♘xe5 64 fxe5 ♗xe5+ 65 ♔g2 b3 66 h8♕ ♗xh8 67 ♖xh8 ♔c5 68 ♔f2 ♔c4 69 ♔e2 b2 70 ♖b8 ♔c3 71 ♔d1 e5 ½-½

D) The Slav Gambit:
3 ♘f3 ♘f6 4 ♘c3 dxc4
5 e4 b5 6 e5 ♘d5 7 a4 e6

As far as I am concerned, 5 e4 just loses a pawn, but some die-hards just keep on playing it! Foremost amongst them is the attacking Swedish player Tiger Hillarp-Persson. So here is one of his typical efforts.

> ### Game 86
> ### Hillarp-Persson - Acs
> *Budapest 1996*

1 c4 c6 2 ♘f3 ♘f6 3 d4 d5 4 ♘c3 dxc4 5 e4 b5 6 e5 ♘d5 7 a4 e6 8 ♘g5!?

The modern line. 8 axb5 ♘xc3 9 bxc3 cxb5 10 ♘g5 ♗b7 11 ♕h5 g6 12 ♕g4 ♗e7 is the old continuation, when Black will follow up with ...♘d7-b6-d5, while White plays for tricks!

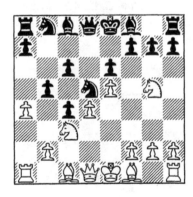

8...♗e7 9 h4!? h6 10 ♘ge4 b4

10...♗a6 immediately is interesting, to avoid weakening the queenside too early. The text leads to absolute chaos, though I think that Black is fine.

11 ♘b1 ♗a6 12 ♕g4 g6 13 ♘bd2 c3 14 ♘c4 ♗xc4 15 ♗xc4 a5 16 h5 g5 17 0-0 ♘d7 18 bxc3 ♘7b6 19 ♗b3 ♘xc3 20 ♘xc3 bxc3 21 ♕e4

♘d5 22 f4 ♖b8 23 ♗a2 ♖b4 24 fxg5 ♕b6! 25 ♗xd5 cxd5 26 ♕f3 ♕xd4+ 27 ♗e3 ♕xe5 28 ♕xf7+

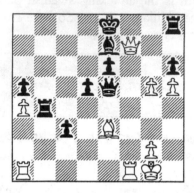

28...♔d8 29 ♖ae1 ♖e4 30 ♗b6+ ♔d7 31 ♖xe4 ♕xe4 32 ♗c5 ♖h7 33 ♕f2 ♗xg5 34 ♖e1 ♕f5 35 ♕e2 e5 36 ♕b5+ ♔c8 37 ♕c6+ ♖c7 38 ♕a8+ ♔d7 39 ♕xd5+ ♔c8 40 ♕a8+ ♔d7 41 ♖d1+ ♗d2 42 ♕d5+ ♔e8 43 ♖f1 ♗f4 44 ♕g8+ ♔d7 45 ♕d5+ ½-½

An amazing game!

E)   3 ♘f3 ♘f6 4 ♘c3 dxc4 5 a4 ♗f5 6 ♘h4!?

This is an interesting little idea that has even been tried by Kasparov.

Here 6...♗c8!? 7 ♘f3 takes us back to square one, but 7 e3 e5 8 ♗xc4 exd4 9 exd4 ♗e7 10 0-0 0-0 11 h3 ♘a6!? 12 ♘f3 ♘c7!, intending ....♗e6, leads to an unclear position. In the next game we see Black allowing the exchange on f5.

> ## Game 87
> ## Savchenko-Ninov
> *Cappelle la Grande Open 1994*

1 d4 d5 2 c4 c6 3 ♘f3 ♘f6 4 ♘c3 dxc4 5 a4 ♗f5 6 ♘h4 e6 7 ♘xf5 exf5 8 e3 ♗d6

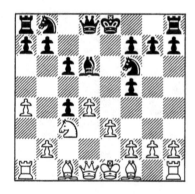

This cannot be bad, but I wonder whether Black cannot develop more effectively. White's basic idea is to play ♕f3, h2-h3 and g2-g4, removing the f5-pawn and thus undermining Black's control of e4. In order to prevent this plan, I would therefore suggest protecting the f5-pawn with ...♕d7, putting the bishop sensibly on e7 and then developing the queen's knight to b4 via a6. This line is of course very similar to Yusupov-Kramnik from the 6 e3 main lines, but since White has taken on f5 so early, allowing Black to prevent e3-e4 with a pawn on f5, rather than his pieces, Black has more flexibility with his piece placement: 8...a5 9 ♗xc4 ♘a6 10 ♕f3 ♕d7 11 h3 ♘b4 12 0-0 ♗e7 is fine for Black.

9 ♗xc4 0-0 10 0-0 ♘bd7 11 a5 a6 12 h3 h5 13 ♕f3 g6 14 e4! ♘xe4 15 ♘xe4 fxe4 16 ♕xe4

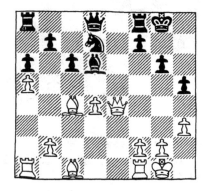

The move ...h7-h5 has rather weakened the black kingside and now ♕xg6+ is threatened.

16...♔g7 17 ♗d2 ♘f6 18 ♕f3 ♘d5 19 ♖fe1 ♗c7 20 ♗xd5 cxd5 21 ♗b4 ♗d6 22 ♗c5 ♗xc5 23 dxc5 ♕d7 24 ♖ad1 ♖ad8 25 ♖d4 ♖fe8 26 ♖xe8 ♕xe8 27 ♕e3 ♕xe3 28 fxe3

White's space advantage gives him a very pleasant rook ending.

28...♔f6 29 ♖b4 ♖d7 30 ♖b6+ ♔e5 31 ♔f2 ♖c7 32 b4 ♔e4 33 ♖d6 h4 34 ♔e2 g5 35 ♔d2 ♖e7 36 c6 bxc6 37 ♖xc6 ♖a7 38 ♖d6 ♖b7 39 ♖b6 ♖a7 40 ♖b8 ♖e7 41 b5 axb5 42 ♖xb5 ♖a7 43 ♖b4+ ♔e5 44 ♖a4 ♔d6 45 a6 ♔c5 46 ♔c3 f5 47 ♖a5+ ♔b6 48 ♖xd5 ♔xa6 49 ♖xf5 ♖g7 50 ♔d3 ♔b6 51 ♔e2 g4 52 ♖h5 gxh3 53 gxh3 ♖a7 54 ♔d3 ♔c6 55 ♖xh4 ♔d5 56 ♖h5+ ♔e6 57 ♔e4 ♖a2 58 ♖h6+ ♔f7 59 ♔f4 1-0

F) 3 ♗f4

With 3 ♗f4 White intends e2-e3, when he will have safely developed his queen's bishop outside the pawn chain.

> *Game 88*
> **Psakhis-Sadler**
> *Megeve (PCA rapidplay) 1994*

1 d4 d5 2 c4 c6 3 ♗f4 dxc4!
Basically winning a pawn.
4 ♘c3 e6 5 e3 b5 6 ♕f3 ♕a5 7 g4 b4 8 ♘e4 b3+ 9 ♘c3 ♗b4 10 ♘ge2 ♕xa2!

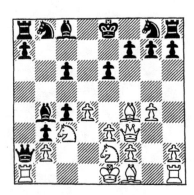

Now after 11 ♖xa2 bxa2 the pawn

queens!

**11 ♖c1 ♕xb2 12 e4 ♘f6 13 g5 e5
14 gxf6 exf4 15 ♕xf4 ♕a3 16 ♕e3
b2 17 ♖b1 ♕a2**

Threatening 18...♕xb1+.

**18 ♔d1 ♕b3+ 19 ♔d2 ♘a6 20 fxg7
♖g8 21 ♕h6 ♗e6 22 ♗h3 ♘c5!**

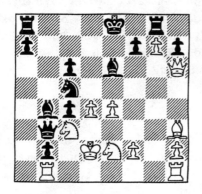

23 ♕xh7 0-0-0 24 d5 cxd5 25 exd5

**♘a4 26 ♔e1 ♗xc3+ 27 ♔f1 ♖xg7
28 ♗xe6+ fxe6 29 ♕e4 exd5 30
♕e6+ ♔b8 31 ♘g3 ♕c2 32 ♔g2
♕e4+!**

Making things safe!

**33 ♕xe4 dxe4 34 ♖hd1 ♖xd1 35
♖xd1 ♗e5 0-1**

Not a good advert for 3 ♗f4!

Summary

The Schlecter variation is a reasonable alternative to 3...dxc4 after 3 ♘c3. However, note that Black can only play this line after e2-e3 by White, as 3 ♘f3 ♘f6 4 ♘c3 g6 5 cxd5 cxd5 6 ♗f4! leads to a superior version of the Exchange variation, which is rather depressing for Black.

White players looking for an offbeat alternative might care to examine 6 ♘h4!?

1 d4 d5 2 c4 c6

3 ♘c3
> 3 ♘f3 ♘f6
>> 4 ♘c3 dxc4 *(D)*
>>> 5 e3 - *game 85*
>>> 5 e4 - *game 86*
>>> 5 a4 ♗f5 6 ♘h4 - *game 87*
> 3 ♗f4 dxc4 - *game 88*

3...e5
> 3...♘f6 4 e3 g6 5 ♘c3 ♗g7 6 ♗e2 0-0 7 0-0 *(D)*
>> 7...b6 - *game 83*
>> 7...dxc4 - *game 84*

4 dxe5 d4 5 ♘e4 ♕a5+ 6 ♗d2 ♕xe5 7 ♘g3 ♘f6 8 ♘f3 ♕d6 9 ♕c2 ♗e7 10 0-0-0 0-0 11 e3 dxe3 12 fxe3 *(D)*
> 12...♕c7 - *game 81*
> 12...♘a6 - *game 82*

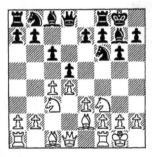
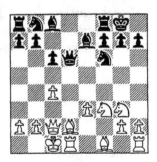

| 4...dxc4 | 7 0-0 | 12 fxe3 |

INDEX OF COMPLETE GAMES

Printed in the USA
CPSIA information can be obtained
at www.ICGtesting.com
JSHW052200100923
47985JS00002B/4

9 781901 259001